JOHN WEBSTER & THE ELIZABETHAN DRAMA

BY

RUPERT BROOKE

British Library Cataloguing-in-Publication Data
A catalogue record for this book is available from the
British Library

NOTE

THIS book was written in 1911-12, and was the "dissertation" with which the author won his Fellowship at King's College, Cambridge, in 1913.

The page references are to Dyce's one-volume edition.

E. M

Contents

Contents

RUPERT BROOKE

Rupert Brooke was born in Rugby, Warwickshire, England in 1887. He was educated at two independent schools in his hometown, and while travelling in Europe prepared a thesis entitled John Webster and the Elizabethan Drama, which won him a scholarship to King's College, Cambridge. Here, Brooke became a member of the Cambridge Apostles and helped found the Marlowe Society drama club.

After leaving Cambridge University, Brooke studied in Germany and travelled in Italy. His first collection of poems was published in 1911, and two years later Brooke became a fellow of King's College, Cambridge. In the same year, he left England to travel in North America, New Zealand and the Pacific islands. He returned home shortly before the outbreak of World War One, during which he took part in the disastrous Antwerp expedition of October 1914.

In February of 1915, while at sea, Brooke septicaemia from a mosquito bite. He died on 23rd April 1915, close to the Greek island of Skyros, aged just 27. He came to public attention soon afterwards, when The Times Literary Supplement quoted two of his five sonnets ('IV: The Dead' and 'V: The Soldier'), and 'V: The Soldier' was read from the pulpit of St Paul's Cathedral on 4th April – Easter Sunday. Brooke's most famous collection of poetry, containing all five sonnets, 1914 & Other Poems, was first published in May 1915.

Brooke's work captured the optimism of World War I's opening months, and expressed an idealism about the conflict that contrasts strongly with the poetry published by later poets such as Wilfred Owen.

PREFACE

I HAVE tried to write a small book about John Webster. That is to say, I have tried to say the truth about him, as much of it as is necessary to enable anyone who reads him to understand him. I have not tried to explain him entirely to anyone who has not read him, though I hope that any person in that condition might get a rough idea of him from this book.

I have tried to explain Webster for a reader, but not to explain him away. So I have endeavoured to keep to my own province, and not to trespass on ground reserved for worthier feet—Webster's. I conceive that there is much that he can explain better than I. So I have, at least, abstained from paraphrasing.

To explain Webster's writings it is first necessary to determine what he wrote, and also such smaller questions as when he wrote it, and how he came to write it. Such questions, the questions of "scientific" literary criticism, I deal with in the Appendices. I have taken some care to get the most probable answers in each case; for there is such a lot of bad logic and fudging on such points in modern literary science, that one always has to go over the whole ground completely for oneself.

When these points are settled, with as much certitude as possible, there are still other points on which it is necessary to have right opinions in order to understand Webster. One must know what a play is; one must know how the Elizabethan drama arose; and one must know what the Elizabethan drama was. I have given a chapter to each of these points; not pretending to cover the whole ground, or to do the work of a whole book; but endeavouring to correct some of the more misleading wrong ideas, and to hint at some of the more important right ones. These chapters, of course, though nominally not about Webster, should be even more important to any understanding of him than the Appendices. And I have given two long chapters to the more direct consideration of what Webster wrote, and what its more usual characteristics are.

The Bibliography is, I think, fairly complete with regard to Webster. I did not think it necessary to make a bibliography of books on the wider subjects.

It may seem, in some cases, as if I contradicted myself in different parts of the book; as, for instance, when I say that it is impossible to understand a play wholly from the text, and later seem to believe that I *do* understand plays wholly from the text. I think I have not really contradicted myself. Part of the business of the earlier chapters is to prevent the necessity of continually repeated qualifications throughout the work. To express my exact meaning on each occasion would have meant covering the page with "in so far as it is possible"s, and "I think"s, and "possibly"s, and "perhaps"s; which makes the style feeble and muffles the idea. I have, perhaps, gone too far in this direction already.

CHAPTER I

THE THEATRE

ANYONE who has read, with any alertness, more than a little of the mass of critical and editorial comments, whether of the last three or of the last three hundred years, upon Elizabethan plays, must often have felt a helpless and bewildered irritation at the absence of any standard or uniform grounds of judgment; both in the critics, and, on inspection, in himself. This is not the place to attempt to lay a deep æsthetic foundation; but I think it will be useful to try and fix the meanings of certain words and phrases, and to give a provisional answer to some of the more important questions.

"What is Art?" is a question which most writers on subjects connected with literature, painting, plays, music, society, or life, are ready with an equal cheerfulness to ask or to answer. They may be right; but to me they seem to make a gigantic, unconscious, and probably unjustifiable assumption. It is quite doubtful, and it is nowadays continually more doubted, whether the word "Art" has properly any meaning at all. But it has so obsessed men's minds, that they start with an inevitable tendency to believe that it has a meaning. In the same way, those who believe in Art are generally inclined to believe in a single object at which all Art, that is to say all the arts, aim: Beauty. It may turn out to be true that both Art and Beauty are real and useful names; but the attitude of mind that assumes that they are is deplorable. The most honest and most hopeful course to pursue, is to say that there are certain kinds of human activity which seem to hang together in classes, such as reading books, hearing music, seeing pictures; and to examine our states of mind while we follow these pursuits, to see how far they are of one kind in each "art," and in all, and whether *all* successful works of art do seem to us to have some quality in common which can be called Beauty.

The situation seems to me as if men had agreed to say "The emotions caused in human beings by pins, walking-sticks, feathers, and crowbars, acting through the tactile sense, are all of one unique kind. It is called Grumph. Pins, etc., are called the grumphs. Grumph is one of the holiest things in this melancholy world," and so forth. And soon they'd say, "But, philosophically, what *is* Grumph?" Then they'd argue. They would come to some conclusion which, as you cannot tickle with a crowbar, would preclude tickling with feathers; and they would excommunicate all those who used feathers for tickling with the formula, "That is not Grumph!" They would write Treatises on any one grumph, on the "Pin-grumph," say, carefully keeping in mind all the time that what they said would have to be more or less true of the other grumphs too. Some would lay great importance on the fact that, as you were tickled with feathers, you were, in a way, also tickled by being beaten with a walking-stick. Others would discover the ferule of the pin, and the quill, shaft, and two vanes of barbs of the crowbar. An Oxford don would arise to declare that all grumph continually approximated to the condition of pins. . . .

I have put the affair, as I see it, in a figure, and with other names, in order to show its unreason more clearly, and far more shortly, than is possible if the prejudice-clad and elusive word "Art" is used. In either case, the sensible reply to it all is, "We have sticks and pins, plays and poems. These we know. These are, as certainly as anything is, real classes of things. Begin from them, and from the emotions they move. And see if thence you climb upwards to Grumph, to Art."

This attitude does, directly or indirectly, shut out various bands of ideas and thinkers; my objections to each of which I could state at length. A short enumeration of these tendencies of mind in viewing questions of "Art" may hint why, psychologically at any rate, they seem to me non-starters. In the first place, I do not admit the claims of anyone who says, "There *is* such a thing as Beauty, because when a man says, 'This is beautiful,' he does not *mean*, 'This is lovely,' or, 'This provokes the cosmic emotion.' There *is* such a thing as Art; because the sentence: 'Pictures, Poetry, Music, etc., are Art,' is not the same as, 'Pictures, Poetry, Music, etc., are Music, Poetry, Pictures *κ.τ.λ.*' " I am not concerned with what men may *mean*. They frequently mean and have meant the most astounding things. It is, possibly, true that when men say, "This is beautiful," they do not mean "This is lovely." They may *mean* that the æsthetic emotion exists. My only comments are that it does not follow that the æsthetic emotion does exist; and that, as a matter of fact, they are wrong.

But the only way to prove them right or wrong is by introspection into our states of mind when we hear music or see pictures.

It has been acutely said that, in philosophy, it is important to give the right answers, but even more important to ask the right questions. So here. Better than to ask "What is Art?" is it to ask "What do you feel before this picture?" "Before that picture?" "Is there anything common between your feelings in these two cases?" "What do you feel in hearing this, and that, piece of music?" "Is there anything common?" and then, "Is there anything common between what you feel before all these pictures and what you feel in hearing all this music?" "And if so, what is it?" "Is it important?" One of the perils attending on those who ask the first question is that they tend, as all men do, to find what they are looking for: a common quality in Art. And also that they tend to exalt what they discover for this quality, above the others that are to be found in any of the arts. People who start in this way are apt to be, practically, a most intolerable nuisance both to critics and to artists; whether it is Art or any one art that they would tie to their rule. Art is Pattern; and a novel that lacks "pattern" is not Art, and therefore bad. Art is the perception of the individual case; so morality plays are illegitimate. Art is the emphasising of the generality; so *Hamlet*, except in so far as the hero represents all neuropaths, is a perverse and downward path from the moralities. Art must be moral; so Shakespeare's sonnets are what Hallam thought them. Art has no connection with morality; so *Paradise Lost* and *Pilgrim's Progress* are, artistically, worthless. A play must display a "development," a tragedy must involve a conflict; music must have a tune; a picture may not tell a story. . . . The list of these perilous and presumptuous *a priori* limitations could go on for ever. Of the wrong ways of approaching the subject of "Art," or even of any one art, this is the worst because it is the most harmful.

But there are other ways in which preconceptions and assumptions about the thing to be looked for mislead, in the consideration of Art. Croce rather naïvely begins by noting that "æsthetic" has been used both for questions of Art and, in general and in accordance with its derivation, for perception. So he sets out to discover what meaning it can really have, to apply to both. He takes it for the one necessary condition a true answer about "Æsthetics" must satisfy, that it shall explain how Art and Perception are both included. Having found such an explanation, he is satisfied.

To take a different side, most of the upholders of the *Einfühlungsästhetik* seem to have founded their view on the experiences of the spectator of certain visual arts, especially painting or architecture. In so far, it is valuable. But when it is contorted to cover the other arts, the result is ludicrous. So those who accept the *Nacherleben* theory, would appear to be extending what is probably true about drama to spheres where it is desperately irrelevant.

It is said that the figure of Helen, whom men have so eagerly followed and sought, was a phantasm, covered by which there lurked, in fact, a knot of mercantile interests of Greece and the Hellespont and the Black Sea; even as, some claim, men who have died for the love of England, or Germany, or Italy, have, in reality, only given themselves for a few rich people. Art and Beauty have proved such delusive

Helens. It is an extraordinary crowd, pouring along diverse roads, that has followed them. The onlooker is moved to amazement and derision. Rossetti's "View Halloo!" was less lonely than he dreamt. More than all illusory goddesses has My Lady Beauty been chased or stalked, as a rule passionately, often irretrievably, "in what fond flight, how many ways and days!" The ingenuity of the chase has been stupendous.

"They sought her with thimbles, they sought her with care;

They pursued her with forks and hope."

The thimble of an *a priori* generalisation has not closed down on My Lady, nor the fork of Dialectic impaled her. For the quest was vain from the beginning. It is that conviction that enables me so cursorily to leave such knight-errants to their task—of "bounding along on the tip of their tail" or "still clutching the inviolable shade," according to the way you regard them. We had best cultivate our gardens of the arts. Then we may turn round one day to discover Beauty at our elbow—if she exists at all. If she doesn't, we shall at least have learnt horticulture.

I can descend, then, with a clear conscience to occupy myself with the single plots of ground called Drama and Tragedy. But first I must deal with two other ways of approaching the question of the arts—for the arts, as human activities, can be classed together, even though there be no such obvious similarity discernible in the states of mind they produce, no "æsthetic emotion." There are some who would view it all from the point of view of the artist. "Art," they say, "is primarily a creative function of the artist; other people may profit, afterwards, if it so happens. Cricket is a game played by twenty-two men, under certain rules: which may or may not be watched by a crowd. This is true, even though the game would not have been played but for the crowd. Art is no more to be explained in terms of the chance result on the spectators than cricket is to be explained in terms of the feelings of the crowd. Art is an amazing creative experience of the artist: what happens to the result of his travail is neither here nor there. A good picture is one in the creating of which the artist had a good state of mind. And the utmost a spectator can hope for is to approximate, in beholding a work of art, to the state of mind the artist had in creating it."

The last sentence, perhaps, expresses a view that need not logically go with the foregoing belief. For the whole position, I do not think it can, ultimately, be refuted. It becomes a question of words, or of the point of view. From where I stand, I seem to see certain activities, and I consider them according to the aspect that seems to me most important. If another man views and describes them from behind, I can only lament it. There are things to be said against him.

Certainly, if importance is to weigh in the matter, the effects on the audience are more important than the state of the artist. He could, cogently, answer that corn is corn, though the most important thing about it is that it goes to make bread. A greater difficulty is the extraordinary variety of experience of the creative artist. Blake thought he was taking down his writings from the dictation of an angel. Some writers solemnly think their things out. Others are "inspired"; or proceed almost by automatic writing. Some are highly excited and irresponsible; others detached, cynical, and calculating. Many artists, it would seem, are never aware of their work of art as a whole, but build it up, patching and revising in little pieces. A play by Beaumont and Fletcher, with the scenes apportioned out, would be difficult to judge by this creative theory. Certainly, if you take the case of a dancer, who can never quite see herself dancing, it seems clear that the important whole connected with this activity is in the state of mind of the spectator.

Another common tendency, a fatal and ridiculous one, is that of the historical school. Both the psychology of the artist and the history of the arts are interesting, and may be valuable, topics of investigation. But it should be clearly recognised that the history of the forms of the arts has no direct connection with the arts as they are. Football originated I in a religious ritual; but it is not, necessarily, religious. The cooking of roast pork arose from the burning of a house; but he would be a foolish gastronomist who, in considering cooking, laid great emphasis on the fundamental element of arson in that art. So there are some who say that the arts originated in a need to let off the superfluous energies of man, not needed to further or secure his livelihood; and therefore are essentially of the nature of play. Others declare that the sexual instinct was at the bottom of the beginnings of the arts, and that all Art is, fundamentally, sexuality. Others again would, for similar reasons, find it a religious activity. To all such we can only reply, "If your historical analysis is true, it is indeed a wonderful world in which we live; but now, in 1912, poetry and football are not sex or religion; they are poetry and football."

There are theatres; places where you see things. The things you see there generally try to represent or imitate reality, and are frequently accompanied by words, in which cases they are called "plays." One of the first and most important distinctions between plays, music, and poetry on the one hand, and pictures and sculpture on the other, is that the element of duration enters into the first group. There is no especial point in a picture at which you begin or end looking at it; no fixed order of sensations. There is just the picture. But the order of sensations which a play should arouse in you is fixed beforehand, and essential. This fact of duration gives theatrical art two features. It can arouse all the emotions that can be got through the consecution of events; and it can employ the succession of emotions in the mind. Both these are important. Take the latter first. It is obvious that, though he may demand certain knowledge in the spectator before the beginning of the play, the artist cannot demand any definite state of mind. He can only claim to be presented with an expectant and fairly blank normal mind. After that he is responsible. And at any moment during the play, his choice of the emotions to arouse is conditioned by the emotions already aroused. Each situation must be planned, each line written, with regard to the effect of what has gone before, not only logically, but psychologically, on the audience. The continuity of the play must be an emotional continuity, even more than a rational one: not necessarily, of course, the *same* emotion continuously, but necessarily *harmonious* ones. I do not mean to suggest that the spectator of a play experiences a number of definite emotions, one at a time, each lasting three seconds, consecutive. His state of mind is complex; and while some perceptions or emotions flash with infinite swiftness through it, others last and colour the contents of subsequent states of mind for some time. It is these last that are most important, but the whole mental and emotional experience has a cumulative effect. It is as if a stream of water of various heat was trickling through a basin. The heat of the water in the basin at any moment would be affected by the heat of the basin, which in turn would be a result of the past heats of all the water that had gone through before. Only, heat is simple, and the succession of emotions and sensations is manifold and complex. The merit and kind of the play, in a sense the play itself, lie in the whole curve of these states of mind. That is the most important thing about plays, to which everything, ultimately, must be referred. I can more easily imagine a play good in which all the characters of the first four acts vanished, and entirely new ones came on in the fifth, with an entirely new plot, so long as the emotions aroused were harmonious, than one in which the successive states of mind clashed.

What a man generally refers to when he speaks of a play, and of the goodness and qualities of it, is a memory of this succession of states of mind, a kind of foreshortened view of it, an emotional *précis* or summary. A good critic is he who can both feel a play perfectly at the time, and sum up its particular taste and intensity perfectly, for his own reference, in this retrospective summary. The process of summarising a play thus involves the abstraction of various, more or less common elements of the successive states of mind the play produces, and the concocting them into one imagined taste or state of mind, "the play." All these summaries are of something the same kind; so the habit of thinking of plays thus leads men to think that there is some common quality in all of them—at least, in all serious ones—"beauty" and a common "aesthetic emotion" always in the mind of all spectators of plays. I believe that honest introspection of one's states of mind during a play, will show that there is no one quality one can call "beauty" in all successful serious plays. If there is any meaning at all in the word "beauty," my emotion at Iago's temptation of Othello, or Lear's "Prithee, undo this button," is in no way a consciousness of beauty; and though there is, perhaps, *something* in my state of mind—the shape of it, so to speak—which is the same when I watch any tragedy, it is only due, I think, to the fact that all tragedies I know have a certain common quality of being partly like life; I do not find this something in my mind when I am watching pure dancing.

A play is good in proportion as the states of mind during the witnessing of it are, in sum, good. The good of these states of mind is, in practice, very much dependent on the pleasurableness of them, and proportionate to it. Much more so than in real life, where the consciousness of virtue makes some unpleasant states good. But pleasure is not a perfect criterion of good, even in the theatre. For a performance that provokes lust would move pleasant states of mind, but not good ones.

If this is granted, the difficulty is: in whom is a play

to move good states of mind, in order to be called good? Obviously, not only in me. A play in Russian might be very good, and yet only bore me, because I couldn't understand it. On the other hand, I do not think it fair to call a play good which can be understood by nobody but the author. Everybody is familiar, in the realm of literature, with the writer who is immensely pleased with his own poem because of the emotions it evokes in him. The phrase "the sun is setting" recalls to him the purple and green glory that moved him to this inadequate expression. But it will not affect anyone else in the same way, so we rightly refuse to call the poem good. Obscurity in an author is, ultimately, a fault. A family of my acquaintance uses a private and peculiar synonym of their own childish invention for "hand," the word "nopen."[1] If one of them wrote a poem containing this word, it would affect *him* very much, because of the aura of associations around it. But the rest of the world would find it meaningless. It would not be a good poem. One is reduced to saying that a good play means a play that would be likely to stir good states of mind in an intelligent man of the same nation, class, and century as the author. It follows that a good Elizabethan play is a play that would have been good in Elizabethan times; and not a play that is good to us, with our different ideas. The two categories coincide to a great extent. But their differences are important.

And it follows that all those literary qualities that answer to *patine* in works of art—quaintness, old-fashionedness, interest as illustrating a bygone age—are irrelevant. I had rather read an interesting book originally worthless, than a fine poem in a language I cannot understand. But it would be misleading to call the former a better book.

Whether the states of mind produced by a play were good or not, must be decided by introspection. The object of most critical enquiries is to discover what sort of effect different things in the theatre have on these states of mind. It is obvious if one examines one's consciousness during a play, that several different classes of object fill and move it. There is sound. Music, or the mere melody of words, impresses and pleases. There is the further literary pleasure of the language, apart from the mere sense; and sometimes there is metre. There is movement, varying from absolute dancing to mere imitation of life. There is, in most theatrical performances the story. And there is the realism of the piece; *i.e.* its value as impressing us with the sense of its reality.

If we exclude pure dancing, all performances in theatres have some value as connected with reality. To discover what it is, one has to consider one of the widest and most important psychological questions connected with the theatre, the question of convention.

To say that one feels the reality of an ordinary ay without

believing it, is a fairly accurate description of one's attitude. It would be better to put it in this way: the feeling of reality, the emotion of conviction, of faith, is a purely psychological one. It is this that plays aim at producing. It is not the same emotion we have in real life. In real life one does not feel "He is really there, talking to me!" One takes it for granted. He *is* there. This is also present to some degree when one is witnessing a play, but it is the negative and less valuable side of the emotion. The former, the positive feeling of reality, does not tend to result in action. The latter does permit of various emotions resulting in action. So there has to be a permanent inhibition of such action; or, to put it in another way, you accept the convention of the actors, the absent fourth wall (on the modern stage), and so on. It was in the want of this inhibition that the wrongness of that Italian's attitude lay, who, at a performance of *Hamlet*, was so wrought upon that he rose from his place in the pit, and shot Claudius. Many find it difficult to understand the attitude of the human mind about such convention. They either say, "Absence of scenery destroys the illusion," or "You must *know* it isn't true." The accepting of a convention means that one says, "Suppose Romans talked English blank verse, then——" and gives oneself to the play; or, to put it another way, one puts a lid on one's knowledge that Romans didn't talk English blank verse. Ignorant of that, one can believe the rest.

This is one of the most natural and deep-rooted instincts in men. We do not want illusion; we only ask that conventions should be made and kept. But it is important that they should be kept. The artist can make any amount of conventions; but, once made, he must not break them. It is obvious in children. A grown-up can say, "Suppose you are a hen, and she is a steam-roller, and I am the King of Portugal," and they will carry the play out with entire acceptance of this, absolute appreciation of the drama ensuing. But if the grown-up breaks from his regal speech and behaviour a moment to address a remark, in his own person, to some outsider or to the steam-roller in its private existence, the grief and dismay of the children is prodigious and unexpected. Observation or memory will assure one that their pain is purely æsthetic. It is what we feel when a dramatist breaks or misuses one of the conventions.

The artist's business, then, is to make these various conventions, and, within them, to impress the spectator as much as possible with the sense of reality. There are many ways of doing this; realism in any one branch—in the chain of events, in the gestures of the actors, in the style of speech, in the truth to life of the characters, or in the scenery—will do to start the feeling of reality, and it will then gather force from the general power of the play. Or there are unrealistic ways of impressing the spectator with reality, through mere literary or theatrical power. It is to be noticed that in some of these things, realism means breaking a convention and setting up a more realistic one, and is consequently comparative. With speech, for example, realism means more realistic speech than one is accustomed to. Robertson's *Caste* was realistic in this direction, in its day. When we had got used to that, Mr Shaw's plays, with their more naturalistic speech, appeared, and seemed to us more realistic. They, in their turn, ring now old-fashioned by the side of more modern plays, the dialogue of which seems to us, for a time, startlingly and triumphantly like real life.

If one keeps in mind the fact that the ultimate classification of plays, for æsthetic purposes, must be by the general tone of the states of mind they evoke, the endeavour to distinguish Tragedy from Comedy, and to define Tragedy, by subject-matter, appears rather misleading. Tragedy may have to have a "hero," it may involve death, it may require a conflict. All we *know* is that, in the two or three varieties of Tragedy we are acquainted with that have hitherto been evolved, these things are generally present. The duty of critics is rather to decide how far it is probable that a play with a hero will evoke deeper "Tragic" feeling than a play without one, and such half-technical and quantitative questions.

The emotions of a spectator are produced in various ways, and through the two channels of the eye and ear.

Performances can mix their appeals through these channels in any proportion. Pantomime can appeal, very powerfully, through the eye alone. A blind man could get a great deal of enjoyment out of some plays. But honest introspection will convince anyone that a very large part of the appeal made by a performance of the kind of play *Hamlet* or *The Duchess of Malfi* is, comes through the eye. Would one rather be blind or deaf at such a performance? It is a comprehensible and common, but dangerous fault, to over-emphasise the importance of the printed text to the whole play. It is true that the romantic halo and additions of beauty to the general lines of the play, came, in Elizabethan plays, very little in the things you could look at; almost entirely in the words. But the story itself was told visually as well as audibly. The Elizabethans were above all men of the theatre, and planned performances. It is important always to keep this in mind when reading their "plays," always to be trying to visualise the whole performance from the text, and to judge it so, and always to look with suspicion on those who judge the text as literature. It may be good literature, sometimes; but it was not primarily that. To judge *The Duchess of Malfi* from the book of the words which we happen to possess is a little like judging a great picture by a good photograph of it. The general plan is given you, and you see all the lines, and shapes, and shading; and you have to supply the colour by an effort of the imagination. Much genuine æsthetic pleasure can be got from this; but no one would be so rash as to assume that, after that, he knew the picture. With plays, people are more presumptuous. But an honest man will sadly have to acknowledge that, in the text, we have only the material for a rough, partial, and hesitating appreciation of *The Duchess of Malfi*; and that this is the truer because it is an Elizabethan play, that is to say, it is written in a language somewhat different from ours, and pronounced differently too, and it was performed in conditions we do not completely know and cannot at all realise. It was composed for an audience accustomed to the platform stage and no scenery; which we can never be. It was composed for the stage, and we judge it as literature; we are only readers. It is right enough to attempt to realise imaginatively Elizabethan plays as plays. It is right enough to admire their great literary merits and their rather accidental power as study-drama. But, after all, we have only the text—and that a not always trustworthy one—one factor of several in the play, a residue, fragments of the whole. We are like men who possess sweet-smelling shards of a jar which once held perfumes, and know how fragrant it must have been; but the jar is broken, and the perfumes lost.

[1] Because it opens.

CHAPTER II

THE ORIGINS OF ELIZABETHAN DRAMA

IT needs the imaginative sympathy of a good anthropologist to understand the real nature of the various progenitors of the Elizabethan drama; and it needs the intuition of a good psychologist to interpret it. Luckily much of the outer history, names, dates, and facts, together with a good deal of understanding explanation, has been given us by such writers as Professor Creizenach, and, above all, by Mr Chambers. Subsequent works, such as *The Cambridge History of English Literature*, merely follow on his lines, sometimes slightly varying relative importances, nothing more. But as one reads the array of facts and the brilliantly powerful generalisations and inductions of Mr Chambers, or the patient condensations of his successors, it is impossible not to feel the full sea of scepticism. Where we have records, do we really understand? It is hard enough, four-fifths of the books now written on them witness, not to be wholly out of touch with the Elizabethans themselves. But they are our brothers and fathers. These others, these white-faced savages who seem to beckon and move in the fog of the Middle Ages or the deeper night behind—what have they to do with us? A surface likeness of name and tongue will not hide their foreignness. Their hearts are different, and distant from ours. They live in another universe. The unconscious worshippers of a vegetation-god, the audience of a *scôp*, the spectators of a miracle-play—what was really in their minds? We triumphantly know that the Feast of Fools was celebrated at Tournai on the eve of Holy Innocents, 1498, that an interlude was given at King's Lynn on Corpus Christi 1385, that the processional religious drama was acted on "pageants," and so forth. But what were the people thinking, as the waggons rolled by or the actors came out? How like was it to an Elizabethan's feeling as he watched *The Tragedy of Byron*? or to ours when we see *The Importance of Being Earnest*? It is absurd to pretend we know.

Such are the misgivings with which the honest student looks back on "the origins of the drama." He can pretend he sees how the "platform-stage" arose, and passed into the "picture-stage"; he can cheat himself into believing he has established the generations of an English dramatic form; but what, in our time and race, is the history of those complicated states of mind the witnessing of *Hamlet* breeds in us—that he dare only wonder.

If he looks beyond the Middle Ages he finds at first more familiar things. Seneca's plays fall recognisable on his modern hearing; and if those were never on the stage, other tragedies and farces which we could, it is imaginable, understand, if not applaud, held the Roman ear. And the modern eye greets even more gladly finer, less recorded, performances. The best taste in Rome loved the intricate exquisite tragedies of the χ€ ιρόσοφοι, the dancers. We glibly call them, allow literary people to call them, the decadent successors of the drama. They may, we can believe now, have awoken passionate ecstasies of emotion, beyond our dreams; but they could not be handed down. These "choreodrames" have perished. So we comfortably fall in with the assumption of those who practise literature, that drama, that queer and monstrous birth, is the God of the theatre. Literary people are very kind to each other; and all-powerful over civilisation. Through them come our history, facts, ideas, and arguments; and so our valuations. We see all things through their mists. The feet of the dancers throb "No!", their heads jerk argument and dialectic to us; we do not heed. We have read of Talfourd, and he will outlive Taglioni. The other arts present themselves naked, to be accepted as they are. Only literature continually weaves laurels, and is for ever crowning herself.

But the arts had always an enemy, especially the arts of

the theatre. The plays we know of and the dancing we ignore were equally threatened by religion, who brought with her the blind forces of asceticism and morality. Any emotional and absorbing view of the universe that throws the value of life over into the next world, naturally regards things of this world as means rather than ends. And so it always tends to combine with and use that deep instinct in human nature, the instinct to treat all things as means, which is called Puritanism. For eighteen hundred years, religion, when it has been strong enough, has persecuted or starved the arts. At times, when it has grown shallow, it has allowed a thin subservient art to flourish beneath it; an art that, ostensibly educating men to be in some way useful, for this life or the next, couldn't help treating them, for a stolen moment, as ends. Such, perhaps, was the pictorial art of the Middle Ages in Italy. But in general the arts have been kept pretty well under, especially the arts of the theatre, creeping slowly out when religion has slept, as in the eighteenth century, or sometimes liberated by such splendid bursts of irreligion as produced the Elizabethan drama in England.

The early fathers of the Church embodied the spirit of religion, knew the Will of God, as clearly in this as in most matters. It is amusing to see that Arius alone went so far as pleading for even a Christian theatre. Here, too, he was a lonely light. All the orthodox makers of Christianity were venomous against *spectacula*. Like children saving up for one great treat, Christians were consoled by Tertullian for the loss of theatres in this world, by the promise of the future spectacle of the exquisite and eternal suffering or richly comic writhing of play-actors and dramatists. The forces of evil triumphed. And the theatre was lost more swiftly and completely than the rest of civilisation, when the double night of barbarism and Christianity settled down over Europe.

The long, long rebirth of the Theatre was a process of roughly the same kind in nearly all European countries. But at present I am chiefly concerned with England. For this country the forces that led to the reappearance of theatrical art and the drama are generally divided into four groups. There were the various travelling minstrels and entertainers; the folk-festivals and folk-plays; the religious drama; and the influence of the classics. The relative importance of some of the earlier fountains of the English drama has been mistaken, through false psychology. Great weight is always laid on the various popular festivals and games, and the unconscious relics of old religions. They are said to be examples of the beginning of mimetic art. If people find a participant in a May-festival taking the name of "The Queen," or a member of a dance assuming a personality with the name of "Ginger-breeches," they stretch delighted fingers, crying, "The origins of drama!" It is an error. It is not true that "the practice which lies at the root of dramatic art and of the pleasure to be gained from it" is "that of pretending to be someone or something else."[1] That is merely what lies at the root of being an actor; and only one of the things even there, as anyone who has known amateur actors can testify. As such, it is but one of the human instincts which, as it happens, enable us to satisfy our love for seeing drama. It has no more to do with "the pleasure to be gained from dramatic art" than the desire for fame which made Keats write, or the desire for expression which made Wagner compose, have to do with poetry or music. They are conditions; at the most, indispensable conditions. The *point* of an art is in the state of mind of the recipient.

"The poet sings because he must;
We read because we will."

Certain pleasant and valuable states of our minds when we see it, are what distinguishes dramatic art. Only such causes as produced them, or earlier forms of them, are directly relevant to a history of the drama or the theatre. Folk-games and festivals, and even folk-drama, have, therefore, it seems to me, nearly no relevance to the history of the English drama.

What is much more important is, of course, the religious drama. Religion, incessantly and half-consciously hostile to the arts, has incessantly and half-consciously fostered them. Every activity of the mind of man is both end and means; and it is as impossible for religion to confine art to be useful, as it is for the pure "hedonist" to make it merely an end. When the first moralist discovered that by putting his advice into a rhymed couplet he interested and impressed the people more, he opened the flood-gates. There soon came along somebody who thought more of the jingle than of the morality. The moralist was powerless to prevent him. Thence follow Martial, Villon, English folk-songs, the Earl of Rochester's play, Baudelaire, and all the abominations of the holy. As the earliest Christian artist sought, in illustrating some incident from Christ's life, to enrich Truth with Beauty, the ghostly, unborn fingers of the Breughels and Félicien Rops guided his brush.

So while Christianity was busily disinfecting the front hall, the most dreadful smells were starting again in the scullery. As early as the fourth century, before she was yet able to triumph completely in the defeat of the pagan theatre, the Church had begun to show forth part of the greatest drama in her universe, by representation, and with all the pomp and wonder of the highest dramatic art. Those who admit the existence of other varieties of theatrical art besides the entirely realistic, must recognise that the state of mind of the spectator of the Mass is strongly æsthetic. Other elements enter, but they combine, not clash, with this. The fact the spectator thinks that what is being represented is true does not make the whole thing undramatic. It becomes a variety of drama, as portrait-painting is a variety of pictorial art, but with less discordant ends than the portraitist must try to serve. That the *importance* of the Mass is quite other than æsthetic is irrelevant. Considered in the light of the states of mind of the spectators of that time, the Mass must have been great drama as surely as Giotto's pictures of the life of Christ were great pictorial art.

Other services and ceremonies of the Church followed in admitting more or less of drama. The history of them, the *Quem quæritis* trope and the rest, had been worked out and often related. The progress from few to many occasions for gratifying the theatrical instinct in men was inevitable. More elaborate as well as more numerous, as the centuries went on, grew the liturgical dramas. They soon began to be transported outside the churches; finally to be played by laymen. More and more scenes from the Bible and from legend were dramatised and performed. They became definitely amusing and interesting for the people, quite apart from the lessons they might teach. Rather too much stress has been laid, naturally, on the great cycles, of Chester, York, Coventry, and elsewhere, that have survived. The accident of their existence must not make us forget that, in church and out, especially out, there were innumerable miracle and mystery plays continually being played through England in the two or three hundred years before Elizabeth. Every little town and village seems to have had them. They were the ordinary food of the theatrical instincts of the people. We cannot understand them now—what there is left. They are far from our ideas of drama, and by our standards they fail. We can see that some of the episodes were funny, that others had pathetic or tragic value, or a queer vitality of characterisation. But the whole seems incoherent, disjointed, and "inartistic." Careful writers go through them, picking out bits of "realistic humour" in one place, and "true literary feeling" in another. It is meaningless; a prattling relation of which parts of these plays appeal to a twentieth-century professor. What *did* those curious mediævals feel when they were watching them? We cannot tell. They may have had as profound and passionate emotions as a play of Ibsen's stirs in us. But as we do not know we cannot affirm that this mediæval drama was good or bad; any more than we can for the Greek drama. Which of the two, for instance, was the greater? It is like a deaf mute having to judge whether Strauss or Mozart is the greater opera-maker. Judging from the librettos, and from watching conductors, he might guess that Strauss was more interesting, Mozart more melodious. . . . He could play with inferences. . . . So (whatever may be claimed by

Greek scholars) must we confess almost complete ignorance about the mediæval drama. Some things can be said. It was certainly narrow; and it cannot have had those qualities of concentration and "dramatic unity," that are necessary for great dramatic art as we are used to know it. But I think there may have been, to the contemporary, more connection and significance in many of these series of plays than the modern will allow. Or rather, the modern sometimes will admit it intellectually, but he does not realise it emotionally. I can conceive the mediæval mind (the exceptional mediæval mind, I admit, for the ordinary childish one must have viewed scene after scene with that transient delight, on a background of reverence, with which schoolboys read *Henry the Fourth*—they find bits very interesting, and they know it's all for their education) tasting in each episode both the episode itself and the whole, in such a way that, finally, that whole loomed out peculiarly solid, majestic, and impressive. The mind would, from its ordinary bent of religious and moral thought, be prepared to receive the play (or cycle) in just this way; and the whole thing would fall into these predestined mental channels with immense accumulating force and power. Just as the *Agamemnon* was meant for, had its significance for, a mind naturally thinking in terms of ὕβρις and ἄτη; so, perhaps, a mediæval series of plays could only find their value in a mind thinking naturally and immediately in terms of the whole Biblical story, theologically interpreted. To the Greek mind the rugs laid down for Agamemnon trailed clouds of horror; to the mediæval the incident of Cain and Abel may have suggested straightly and sincerely, in a way we could never feel it, the entire ancestry of Christ, or the meaning of a later greater sacrifice, and may have illuminated and caught light from the whole tremendous process of the working out of the Will of God. I do not know if the mediæval cycles consciously tried to produce an effect of this kind, or if they ever succeeded, enough to make them worthy, in their narrow kind, to stand by the great dramatic products of other styles and other ages. I only suggest that, æsthetically, they may have been of this nature. It is a method, this subordinaing the parts to the whole, in such a way that the parts have no necessary connection with each other except through the whole, that is strange to us who are used to "plots" that centre about one incident or situation, or one or two characters. In it Time or Fate are the protagonists. It might have, but never did, come off in those dreary chronicle-plays, that increase the desolation of the early Elizabethan drama. It is a method that has been used in later days with greater success. Wagner in *The Ring* gets something of this effect. And Hardy in *The Dynasts* and Schnitzler in *Der Junge Medardus* have used these apparently disconnected, episodic scenes, with or without commentary, for a resultant whole as different from them as a face is from its parts, nose, eyebrows, ears and the rest. They show you a street-scene, some friends, two lovers—all irrelevant—and you know Vienna of 1809. Or they pick out, perhaps, and light up, a few disconnected objects on the stream of time, and you are suddenly, terribly aware of the immense black un-returning flood, sliding irrevocably between darknesses.

Such a method, however, if it existed in mediæval times, did not influence the Elizabethan drama. The disconnected narrative form was indeed an Elizabethan inheritance from mediæval religious drama; but merely as narrative. The narrative was transferred from sacred subjects to historical; the line is pretty clear. The chronicle-plays, indeed, appear to be artistically a retrogression. In incidents and in the whole they are more pointless. The loose narrative style, the limber and many-jointed acts, and the habit of bringing everything on the stage, lasted in the plays of the great period—the beginning of the seventeenth century. Besides this, the miracle and mystery plays gave little to the Elizabethan drama. They handed on the possibility of tragedy and comedy; but that gift was not needed. They bequeathed, too, a certain rather admirable laxity and vagueness with regard to locality in drama; and a tiresome, confusing tendency to make plays illustrate a moral, a tendency which fitted in only too well with the theory of Elizabethan times; less, fortunately, with its practice.

These miracles and mysteries in their various forms lasted, in country parts at least, to overlap with the Elizabethan drama. But there was another form of the religious play which actually formed the chief link with the later style, the morality. It was a late growth, and it rather superseded the miracles and mysteries. It was aided, though not originated, by the revival of learning and moral fervour that followed the Renascence and accompanied the Reformation; and, coming at this time, it soon widened from merely religious ideas to all kinds of secular intellectual notions. It is distinctly of the age of Protestantism, and so we can understand it, better at least than its predecessors, in the same way that we can understand Erasmus. It deals less with God and more with man and the abstractions that were thought to surround his life. By such strange ways the arts came home. Moralities and moral interludes, in their turn, could have produced (and did produce in *Everyman* at least) great drama in their kind. But again, it was a narrow kind. Had that tide flowed on unchecked, we might now look back on an immense English Drama of types and personifications, a noble utterance, in this narrow sort, of all the human desires and dreams and interpretations of life for centuries. The crown and glory of the English theatre would have been Milton—*Comus*, even now, is, in disguise, the most noble example of morality. We

might have achieved the most solemn and noble drama of
the world—a nobility astonishingly different from the glory
we have achieved, its direct opposite. For the transformation
of the morality into the Elizabethan play was a complete
reversal of direction. The whole point of the former is
that it deals with the general; you find all your experience
drawn together and illuminated; you are pervaded, rather
than shaken, with the emotion of the philosopher who sees
the type through the individual, Love beneath the lover.
The latter gives you the particular; some definite person or
circumstance so poignantly that you feel it; the reality for
those vaporous abstractions, not Love but William in love,
not Death but some fool, rather untidily, dying. The one
shows you Everyman, the other Hamlet. Each way is good;
but to go from one to the other, is as if English art twenty-
five years ago had suddenly swung from Watts to Whistler.

Those who are fond of comparing epochs in history with
stages in the life of a man will be pleased to liken the mediæval
miracles and mysteries to the narratives that delight children,
the period of the moralities to that invariable love of youth for
generalities and proverbial wisdom—for Love, Death, Fate,
Youth, and all the wonderful heart-lifting abstractions—and
in the Elizabethan's climb to that chief abode of art, the heart
of the individual, they will find the middle-aged turning,
with the strength as well as the bitterness of agnosticism,

to all that one can be certain of, or, after a bit, interested in, men, women, places, each as a "special case." But if the moralities are taken on their own merits and not as a step in a process, it is doubtful whether they are, artistically, an advance on miracles and mysteries. Dodsley's point, that they were a better kind, as giving the author greater freedom, enabling him to invent his plots, has been often repeated. There is not much in it. The Greeks and most of the Elizabethans did not, in that sense "invent" their plots. In the Christian stories and legends the greatest dramatist could have found enough to last him a life-time. Any old story does for the framework of a play. The moralities, in fact, in putting the dramatist to the trouble of inventing a "plot," rather tended to divert his attention from more important things. In other ways, however, they did widen the ground for the dramatist; and in making plays more wholes and less narratives, and insisting on dramatic unity, they prepared very efficiently for the Elizabethan kinds of drama. It might, indeed, have been better if their legacy of dramatic unity had been more strictly observed. Their other characteristic, of thinking in types and abstractions, instead of individuals, had a longer influence, of no very healthy kind, than is at first obvious. Dr Faustus is only Everyman, or at least Every-philosopher, with a name and a university degree. And there was also a moralising effect; which is not quite the same thing. An art which proceeds by personifications of abstract ideas need not moralise, though in this instance it nearly always did. A modern morality in which the characters were Evolution, The-Survival-of-the-Fittest (his comic servant), Man, and the various Instincts, might be very impressive without conveying any moral at all. The Elizabethan drama, however, started with the burden of this idea among others, that a play rather ought to specify a moral generalisation. It took some time to shake it off.

The third more or less dramatic activity through the Middle Ages was provided by the minstrels and strolling entertainers of various kinds. The ancestors of these were on the one hand the actors of Rome, the *mimi*, who, when the theatres ceased, took to wandering about and giving entertainments, and on the other the more reputable and probably less dramatic Teutonic *scôp*. These minstrels were a great feature of the whole mediæval period, but their importance in the history of the theatre has always been under-estimated. There are two reasons, I think. One is that their performances have left very little record. The history of religious drama can be traced fairly fully. Minstrels of all kinds may have been giving unceasing dramatic entertainments throughout Europe during the same centuries. We have nothing to say about it. There are no traces to investigate, no written text of the performances to comment on. So, as we continually hear of the religious performances and never of these others, we insensibly grow to attach great importance to the former and to omit the latter altogether in our view. The second reason lies in the error in psychology I have discussed. It is supposed that, while any band of rustics dressing up is relevant to the history of drama, no entertainment given by minstrels is, unless it is full-blown realistic acting. I think that careful consideration of the imagined states of mind of a mediæval, or indeed of a modern, audience, will show that the theatrical emotion begins far before that. Even a single minstrel reciting a tragic story seems to me nearer to evoking it than many apparently more "mimetic" activities. And directly he introduces any representation or imitation—as reciters always tend to do—drama is, in embryo, there. I think it is certain that a single performer can produce all the effects of drama, by representing, conventionally, several characters in turn. Mlle. Yvette Guilbert does it. You get from her the illusion of seeing, with extraordinary insight and vividness, first the prisoner of Nantes, and then the gaoler's daughter, quite as much as you would in an opera. The thing can go further. I myself have seen a mere amateur represent at one time and in his one person two lame men, each lame in a different way, walking arm-in-arm, with almost complete realism. And when it comes to dialogues and *estrifs* between two or more performers, it seems to me absurd pedantry, a judging by forms instead of realities, to deny the presence of drama.

In any case, the *mimi* went into the darkness, at the end of Rome, performing plays; and the same class reappears, performing plays, as soon as we can discover anything about them, centuries later. The influence of the farces these wanderers were playing towards the end of the middle ages, on early English comedy, is more or less recognised. I think it is very probable they had a great influence also on tragedy and on drama as a whole. Some of them, it is known, used to perform puppet-plays wherever they went. The importance of these in keeping drama and the taste for tragedy and comedy alive in the hearts of the people is immense. These strolling professional entertainers took their part also in other kinds of dramatic performances. We find them helping in folk-plays and festivals; and when the religious plays were secularised, they often appear as aiding the amateurs. Indeed, the "interlude," the favourite dramatic form which develops out of the secularised religious plays, and which led straight to the Elizabethan drama proper, fell largely into the hands of the "minstrels." About that time they were reinforced, and rivalled, by the various local companies of actors who began touring in a semi-professional way. They were also strengthened during the fifteenth and sixteenth centuries by being enrolled in the service of various great lords. Under both popular and aristocratic circumstances these professionals, after severe competition with amateurs during the first part of the sixteenth century, settled, some of them, into theatres, and became the actors of the Elizabethan drama. Their importance in this light is obviously very great. But their true position can be guessed by inspecting Mr Chambers' appendices of mediæval plays and Mr Tucker Murray's more recent researches. It was that they were responsible for continual dramatic performances of every kind throughout England. How good or bad these were we cannot tell. The forces of religion opposed them, with varying vigour at different periods, and probably succeeded in degrading them to a low level. But they must have prepared the mind of the people to expect certain things in tragedy or comedy; and they may account for various aspects of Elizabethan plays that neither the religious nor the classical influence explains.

By the middle of the sixteenth century, then, the drama was in an inchoate condition. Interludes of all kinds, moral, religious, controversial, and farcical, were being played by all sorts of audiences, besides the rough beginnings of popular tragedy and comedy, and many survivals of the old religious plays. In the sixties the real Elizabethan drama began; and one of the chief influences in working the change was the classical one. It came from above, and from amateurs. It was started, it is noteworthy, by people with a fixed, conscious, solemn, artistic aim. They wanted to have tragedies in the real classical way; so they imitated, queerly enough, Seneca! English literature has always been built on a reverent misunderstanding of the classics. Anyhow, anyone is good enough to be a god. The worst art has always been great enough to inspire the best. The iron laws of heredity do not affect literature; and Seneca may father Shakespeare as Macpherson fathered the Romantic Movement.

The dates of the Senecan movement in Italy, France, and England have been elaborately worked out. They do not concern us now. The influence of Seneca, and, vaguely, what was thought to be the classical tradition, in accordance with the misunderstood laws of Aristotle, came primarily by two streams, through Italy and France. *Tancred and Gismunda* was influenced by the Italian Senecans; Kyd translated Gamier. Italy, of course, the romantic home of all beauty and art, had the most influence. But culture came from France. The English began translating Seneca for themselves in the sixties and seventies. As far as can be seen, the position in the eighties, when Marlowe and Kyd were about to fling English tragedy as we know it shouting into the world, was that the popular stage was scarcely touched at all by this classical, Senecan movement; the children's companies and ordinary court plays were only partly and patchily affected;

but private performances in the Inner Temple and Gray's Inn had proudly and completely adopted the Senecan (or, generally, classical) style. As these were often given before the Queen, they had great influence in spreading the impression that this type of tragedy was the highest, the only type intellectual and cultivated people could aspire to. The Senecan boom did not leave much directly to Elizabethan drama; far less than is generally made out. It left perhaps a ghost tradition, the much-advertised and over-valued "revenge motive," and the tendency to division into five acts. But indirectly it had value in tightening up the drama, pulling the scattered scenes which appeal to the English, a little, but not too much, into one play. And it was of vast use as an ideal. It enabled the dramatists to write for their audiences but above them. It set the audiences an æsthetic standard, shook them into artistic morality. Left to itself, this movement would have, and did, become academic, cold, dead. But Fulke Greville, Alexander, even Ben Jonson, did not get the full benefit of it. The best of it, and the best of the popular stage, were torn out, combined, and revitalised by Kyd and Marlowe. Towards that the times were ripening. The drama was getting a standing, the first important step. It was at once popular and fashionable. And, though a few Puritan fanatics had started a protest, the main mass of the people were against them. That gradual depletion of the theatre-audiences which took place during the next century, when *bourgeois* democracy slowly became one with Puritanism, had not commenced. The establishment of fixed theatres in London must have raised the level of the performances; and, the second important step, it was educating and preparing an audience. For an audience must be trained and trained together, as much as a troupe of actors. It is equally one of the conditions of great drama.

[1] C.H.E.L., vol. v. p. 28.

CHAPTER III

THE ELIZABETHAN DRAMA

THERE are many ways of considering a subject like the Elizabethan drama. You can take the plays by authors. Naturally, it is one of the best ways; and it is the only way that was employed up to quite recently. To use that method alone leads to queer blindnesses. And it is apt to end in the "our Shakespeare" business, an easy and unprofitable way of taking art.

Then there is division by subjects, the method of Professor Schelling and of Polonius. This counteracts the evils of the first way; but it is often rather unmeaning. *Measure for Measure* gets grouped with the "Romantic Comedies." That is to say, the fault is in the unreality of the classes. They should rather be grouped by taste. An arrangement under purely fanciful names would be more practical. *Love's Labour Lost* would go with Lyly under "Court Butterfly"; *Measure for Measure* might jostle *The Fawn* or *Hamlet* in the "Brass-on-the-Tongue" sub-division of the "Leaves-a-Taste-in-the-Mouth" group.

And there is the reader's way, Lamb's way, of just picking out the best plays. It has a lot to be said for it.

All three methods, and others, have their complemental merits. But I think the most useful way of surveying material like this is by a combination, in the following way. One should divide the plays, roughly chronologically, according to their style or taste, the general *Stimmung* of them, with a certain reference to authorship, and distinct emphasis on the merits and possibilities of the various styles. For though, of course, when you stop to consider any particular part, these questions of influence, "schools," styles, periods, and the rest, immediately sink into their proper subordination, yet, for a rapid survey, they *do* correspond to certain realities. It *is* important to know that a writer was aiming at a certain atmosphere, or influenced by it. And some of these atmospheres, and these aims, *are* much healthier for art than others. At any rate, I think that to explain what Webster's plays really are, it is necessary to show where they fit in with the rest of the Elizabethan drama. And as I do not know of any survey of this drama that seems to show the main outlines right, especially with regard to comparative goodness—the scientific literary historian makes every play equally dull, the Swinburnian critic makes every author equally supreme—I shall try to give, very briefly, my own views.

Soon after Lyly began to breathe into comedy (with which I am not concerned) a movement that was near to being life, and a prettiness that was still nearer beauty, Kyd and Marlowe blew life, strength, and everything else into tragedy. To say that they grafted the energy of popular tragedy on the form of classical, would be to wrong by a soft metaphor their bloody and vital violence. It was rather as if a man should dash two dead babies together into one strident and living being. Kyd, of course, does not really stand by Marlowe. But he seems further below him than is fair, because Marlowe's genius was more literary, and so lives longer. Both brought light and life to tragedy. Kyd filled Seneca's veins with English blood. He gave his audience living people, strong emotions, vendetta, murder, pain, real lines of verse, and, stiffly enough, the stateliness of art. He thrilled a torch in the gloom of the English theatre. Marlowe threw open a thousand doors, and let in the sun. He did it, in the prologue to *Tamburlaine*, with the superb insolence and lovely brutality of youth. His love of the body, his passion for the world of colour and stuff, his glorious atheism, "giantism 'gainst Heaven," were trumpets in that morning. The blood still sings to them. Marlowe is less representative, stands clearer of his period, than almost any Elizabethan. He was of no school, had no followers. Others, Shakespeare for instance, caught something of his trick of blank verse, or tried a play or two in his manner. But there was no body of drama that partook of the atmosphere of ferocious, youthful, passionate tragedy that distinguishes Marlowe's work. He stands rather, in his joy of the world, and irreligion, as the herald of the whole age, and of that short song of passion it could utter before the beginning of the night. His loneliness is explicable. It was not only that no contemporary was old and great enough to take all he had to give. But his dramatic method was unique. He was not a dramatist in the way the others were. He was—in this something like the young Shakespeare, but far more so—a lyric writer using drama. "Plot" does not matter to him. Each scene he works up into an intense splendid lyric. They are of different kinds, but put together they have unity. The whole is a lyric drama. No one else, except, conceivably, Webster, in a slight degree, used this artistic method. Marlowe was an extreme *pointilliste*. He produced his whole effect by very large blobs of pure colour, laid on side by side. The rest were ordinary semi-impressionists, with a tale to tell. Only Webster more than rarely achieved expressionism.

One other gift Kyd and Marlowe, especially Marlowe, gave their contemporaries; blank verse. Before them was the Stone Age; they gave the poet a new weapon of steel. Marlowe was drunk on decasyllabics, the lilt and clang and rhetoric of them. How he must have shouted, writing each line of

Tamburlaine! It all fits in with the rest of this outburst of true great tragedy in the eighties. But it was only an outburst of youth; and the sentimentality and tediousness of youth had to be gone through before the best times could be won. The rest of the history of the drama during this century is mainly concerned with the histories and chronicles. Something—it may have been the Spanish Armada—made the audiences demand this dreary kind of play. Their other cry (I have only space to discuss the best audiences and plays) seems to have been for a slight kind of romantic comedy. They swallowed everything, of course, as at all periods of this eighty years. But these two types of play, were, perhaps, most prominent.

Critics have always idiotically thought it their duty to praise these histories; partly because Shakespeare, in obedience to popular demand, wrote some; partly because they are supposed to exemplify the patriotism of the Elizabethans, and we are supposed to enjoy that patriotism. These chronicle-plays fit in, it is not very clear how, with Drake, Hawkins, and the rest of the "island story." And those numerous literary or dramatic critics who do not care for literature or the drama, nod their sentimental approbation. It sounds too fantastic for truth, but it is true, that the ultimate defence of Elizabethan drama offered by many writers on it, is that it holds up so faithful a glass to the "bustling, many-sided life of that wonderful time." Such wretched antiquaries beam mild approval on these new proofs of the Elizabethan's interest in his country's history.

It must be clearly decided that these histories were a transient, dreary, childish kind. They preserved the worst features of Elizabethan drama in their worst form; the shapelessness, the puerility, the obvious moralising, the succession of scenes that only told a narrative, the entire absence of dramatic unity, the mixture of farce and tragedy that did not come off. I do not mean (for the moment) to say that the Elizabethan type of play was bad, as such; only that when done in this form it was silly and without value. One or two tragedies that were written in the form of histories are some good; *Richard II* and *Edward II*. And, of course, in his worst efforts Shakespeare always leaves touches of imagination and distinction. But as a whole these histories are utterly worthless.

Something similar is the case with the romantic comedies. Neither in themselves, nor as a sign of the taste of the times, have they much value. Occasionally they achieve a sort of prettiness, the charm of a stage-spring or an Academy allegory of youth. And Shakespeare threw a pink magic over them. But it should be left to girls' schools to think that the comedies he obligingly tossed off exist in the same universe with his later tragedies. The whole stuff of this kind of play—disguises, sentimentality, girls in boys' clothes, southern romance—was very thin. It might, perhaps, under different circumstances, have been worked up into exquisite, light, half-passionate comedy of a limited kind. It did not achieve even this success.

There are one or two isolated good plays of indefinable genus, like *A Midsummer Night's Dream*. But on the whole this period of silliness or undistinguished prettiness between the great years of Marlowe (*c*. 1588) and the wonderful, sultry flower-time of the next century, is only redeemed by one kind of drama that was seriously trying to move serious artistic emotions. It is a kind that is despised by the refinement of modern criticism, condemned by the word "crude"; what is called "domestic tragedy." These indigenous plays, descendants probably of unknown myriads of popular tragedies in England, were nearly always dramatisations of recent occurrences. Some are bad, and all are as "crude" as life. But they kept people in touch with realities, with the brutality of blood and death. The theatre might so easily have gone irrevocably soft during these years. They kept it fit for the tragedy that was to come; and they profoundly influenced that tragedy for the eighty years of "Elizabethan drama." But it was at this time that they were especially common. The only long study of the subject[1] contains a list of the plays of this nature. There are twenty-four known; fourteen of them occur in the period 1592-1603, two earlier, eight later. It is noteworthy that of the three best we know, one, *Arden of Feversham*, comes at least at the beginning of the period, almost in Marlowe's time, the second, *A Woman Killed with Kindness* (Heywood's best play), comes right at the end, in the golden years of the next century, and the third, *A Yorkshire Tragedy*, is generally dated as right in the middle of that great age, in 1605.

For there was a period—1600-1610 are the rough inside limits—that stood out an infinity above the rest. Nearly all the good stuff of Elizabethan drama was in it or of it. Except in comedy, there are only the lonely spring of Marlowe and the Indian summer of Ford outside it. And it is not only that it was Shakespeare's great time. That is partly both cause and effect, and our great good fortune.

The whole age, in drama and beyond, was alive with passion and the serious stuff of art. Nor was it only that so much of great merit was produced in this short time. Nearly all the work of the period shared, apart from its goodness, in a special atmosphere. It is extremely important to recognise the absolute distinctness and supreme greatness of this period, its sudden appearance and its swift and complete end. There is only space here to hint at its characteristic features. It was heralded (poetry is generally a few years ahead of drama) by Shakespeare's sonnets, and the poems of Donne—who, in spite of Ben Jonson, did not write all his best things before 1598. Poets, and men in general, had reached a surfeit of beauty. The Renaissance joy in loveliness, the romantic youthfulness of the age, the wave of cheerful patriotism, all passed at the same time. Boyhood passed. Imagination at this time suddenly woke to life. Its flights were to the strangest corners and the pitchiest barathrum of the deep. Intellect was pressed into the service of the emotions, and the emotions were beaten into fantastic figures by the intellect. The nature of man became suddenly complex, and grew bitter at its own complexity. The lust of fame and the desire for immortality were racked by a perverse hunger for only oblivion; and the consummation of human love was observed to take place within the bright, black walls of a flea. It seemed as though all thought and all the arts at this time became almost incoherent with the strain of an inhuman energy within them, and a Titanic reaching for impossible ends. Poetry strove to adumbrate infinity, or, finding mysticism too mild, to take the most secret Kingdom of Heaven by storm. Imagination, seeking arcane mysteries, would startle the soul from its lair by unthinkable paradoxes. Madness was curiously explored, and all the doubtful coasts between delirum and sanity. The exultations of living were re-invigorated by the strength of a passionate pessimism; for even scepticism in that age was fecund and vigorous, and rejoiced in the whirling gloom it threw over life. The mind, intricately considering its extraordinary prison of flesh, pondered long on the exquisite transiency of the height of love and the long decomposition that death brings. The most gigantic crimes and vices were noised, and lashed immediately by satire, with the too-furious passion of the flagellant. For Satire flourishes, with Tragedy, at such times. The draperies of refinement and her smug hierarchy were torn away from the world, and Truth held sway there with his terrific court of morbidity, scepticism, despair, and life. The veils of romanticism were stripped away; Tragedy and Farce stood out, for men to shudder or to roar.

In a time so essentially healthy for all that is fine in man, and especially in his arts, it is no wonder that the best in a great many different styles was being done. But each of these bests has some trace of the spirit of the times. Chapman, for instance, was doing his finest serious work. *Bussy D'Ambois* comes near the beginning of the period, the two Byron plays later on, *The Revenge of Bussy* at the end. Chapman is of the time in his intellect, but not in his emotions. His devotion to the "Senecal man," and the archaistic austerities of his style, are his alone. He was too moral for the morbidity of the others, and too dispassionate for their gloom. He was not interested in the same feelings. But his mind delighted in the same intricate convolutions of thought and half-absurd, serious paradoxes. And occasionally he strikes into, those queer horrors that delighted Donne and Marston, and Tourneur and Webster and Shakespeare. He never made a great success of drama, because he thought in a literary and rhetorical rather than dramatic way. He is good reading, but he would not be good seeing. There are two ways of displaying character in literary drama, through words and through action. Chapman has only the first; Webster had something of the second too. Webster revered Chapman, but he was not much influenced by him. Ben Jonson also is at first sight apart from the spirit of this period, although his best work belongs to it. His theories of tragedy prevented him from contributing to the Marston-Tourneur-Webster type of play. He would have condemned the atmosphere which is their great virtue as unclassical. They probably did so—we know Webster did so—themselves. But he is very relevant, all the same. In the first place that attitude of professionalism in art and respect for the rules which he stood for all his life, was a great factor in raising the dignity of drama and the standard of the dramatists. But Jonson's chief influence and achievement in English drama was in founding the Comedy of Humours; and both this kind of play and his examples fit in with the rest of the time. It is so far from sentimentalism, such a breaking with romantic comedy, this boisterous personification of the "humours" of mankind, with its heartiness and rough strength. It has the life of the time. Jonson brought comedy home to England and to men. The characters in his comedy were not complete men, but they were human caricatures, the right stuff for farce and loud laughter. Their vigour grew amazing under his handling. In result he gave the stage the best comedies of all the age. Their coarse splendour of life was never approached till twenty years or more had passed, and his influence again was strong, in the work of some of his "sons." There, comedy survived the floods of sweetness under which tragedy utterly perished.

But if *Epicoene* and *The Alchemist* are admirably complementary in this Pantheon to *Sophonisba* and *The Duchess of Malfi* and *Timon of Athens* and *Macbeth*, other works of Jonson are something more. It is probable that the additions to the 1602, *The Spanish Tragedy*, are Jonson's. If so, he is responsible for some of the finest scenes of imaginative horror in that literature. These few pages (written in 1600) contain most of the terror and splendour of the next ten years. They set the tune unfalteringly. And Jonson did also what Marston never quite succeeded in doing, he wrote a good comedy which had more of this seventeenth century pungency in it than any tragedy, a comedy that is a real companion to the tragedies of Webster. The mirth of Tourneur is horrible; Languebeau Snuffe poises one sickly between laughter and loathing. *Volpone* is like one long laugh of Tourneur's, inspired by a tenfold vitality. It is amazing, one of the few complete works of genius of the Elizabethan age. The hot cruelty and vigorous unhealthiness of it! Its very artistic perfection is frightening and exotic.

But perhaps the main current of strength in the drama during these years, and certainly the most important for this essay, is that which ran through Marston and Tourneur to Webster. Donne was in connection with it, too, from the side of poetry and thought. The relation of Shakespeare with the whole of this period, of which he, then at his greatest, was, to our eyes, the centre, is curious. His half-connections, the way he was influenced and yet transmuted the influences, would require a good deal of space to detail. But in this, his "dark period"—whatever it was, neuralgia, a spiritual crisis, Mary Fitton, or literary fashion, that caused it—he was not unique or eccentric in the *kind* of his art. His humour was savage, he railed against sex, his tragedies were bloody, his heroes meditated curiously on mortality. It was all in the fashion. His gloom was not conspicuous in the general darkness. He had, in *Hamlet* especially, affinities with this Marston-Webster group. His terrific and morbid studies of madness influenced theirs.

Marston is one of the most sinister, least understood, figures in Elizabethan literature. More than anybody else, he determined the channels in which the great flood of those ten years was to flow. His life was curious. He started, like so many of them, by writing vivid, violent, crabbed satire. He went on to play-making, which he pursued for eight years with great success. He was much admired and very influential, but he always presented himself to the world with a typical, passionate ungraciousness. At the end of the eight years he renounced the applause that he so liked disliking, and went into the Church. He had a queer lust for oblivion. His tombstone bears *Oblivioni Sacrum*. It was his personality rather than his powers that was the most stupendous thing about him. To us he seems nearly always just not to bring his effects off; but his contemporaries, whatever they thought, could not escape him.

He started the movement of this period by resuscitating the old blood-and-thunder revenge tragedy. It was precisely what was needed, but he clothed it with his own peculiar temperament of violent and bloody satire. It was this that really attracted the writers of the time. He gave them several plays steeped in it, both comedies and tragedies by the ordinary classifications, really only of one kind. The horror and inhuman violence of his laughter lit up those years like a vivid flash of lightning. He is responsible for that peculiar *macabre* taste, like the taste of copper, that is necessary to, if it is not the cause of, their splendour. But he was of his age in its strength as well as in its morbidity.

"My God's my arm; my life my heaven, my grave To me all end."

says Syphax. Chapman could scarcely have equalled the strong nobility of it.

Marston's chief passion was for truth. He preferred it if it hurt; but he loved it anyhow. It comes out in the snarling speculations and harangues of those satirical malcontents he was so fond of. He bequeathed the type to Tourneur and Webster. For Marston, who was a wit and a scholar and a great poet, was pre-eminently a satirist. It was because he loved truth in that queer, violent way that some men do love, desirous to hurt. It fits in with his whole temperament— vivid, snarling, itching, dirty. He loved dirt for truth's sake; also for its own. Filth, horror, and wit were his legacy; it was a splendid one. Some characters too, besides the Malcontent, were his offspring. He may have originated the heroine who was wicked or non-moral, fascinating and not a fool. It was a type that was refreshingly and characteristically prominent in the great period. Cleopatra, Vittoria, the Insatiate Countess—the womanly heroine fades to a watery mist when they sweep on. Marston is more famous for what he lent than what he had, but what he had is superb.

Of Tourneur (the dates of whose play, or two plays, are most uncertain) less need be said. Nowadays he is thought better than Marston. He is really far his inferior. He does not shock you in the same way by hideously violent contrasts. He is more level; he is more conscious of his purpose; and it may be true that none of Marston's plays is as good as his (if he did write *The Revenger's Tragedy*). But Marston is the greater genius. Still, Tourneur with his brilliant and feverish morbidity carried on the line. He did not influence Webster so deeply as Marston did. It was natural. He used for the most part external horrors for horror's sake. He could not comprehend those horrors of the mind and soul that Shakespeare and Webster knew and Marston glimpsed. But Tourneur was in sight of the end of greatness; the period of horrors was coming to a close.

For Beaumont and Fletcher were beginning their fatal reign. At first cleanness and greatness were still there; and while Beaumont lived the degradation could not go far, for he had a sense of humour and satire. His sentimentality had strength beneath it. He could handle metre like an Elizabethan. None of these things could be said of Fletcher. He had only a kind of wit, a kind of prettiness, and an inelastic sub-variety of the blank verse line. But for the first six years or so, from 1608-1614, they, principally Beaumont, were doing fairly good work. It is good work of a fatally new kind, but the vices of the new have not yet grown to their full. To these years *The Faithful Shepherdess, The Knight of the Burning Pestle, Philaster*, and *The Maid's Tragedy* belong; but drama was on a downhill course.

It has sometimes been said that the most extraordinary gap in the history of our literature, or of any other, is the one between the beginning and the end of the seventeenth century. That little break of twenty years in the middle seems at first sight to have made a tremendous difference. Dryden's inability to understand Shakespeare and his fellows is a common-place; and one can see how inevitable it was from their minds. The cataclysm of the Civil War, social changes, and the sojourn of the generation abroad, are generally held responsible. (Sir George Etherege saw the *premières* of Molière in Paris.) Closer inspection shows the wrongness of this view. Anyone familiar with the life, literature, and drama of court circles just before the outbreak of the Civil War, will realise that the extraordinary thing is how like they are to the products of the Restoration period. There was no gap. Sir John Denham's *The Sophy* (1641) is almost indistinguishable from a Restoration play. The true gap is far more remarkable and far earlier. It is hidden by over-lappings, but its presence is obvious about the year 1611. Five years before that, England was thunderous with the most glorious tragedy and the strangest passion. Five years after that, Fletcher and the silly sweetness of tragi-comedy were all-powerful. The path, unmistakeably the same path, led on and down, through Massinger and Shirley. Five years before that, the intellect and the imagination had been dizzily and joyfully up-borne on that wit Chapman thinks so fine:—

"Your wit is of the true Pierian spring,

That can make anything of anything."

It was exhilarating, if sometimes irritating. The wit that succeeded it was Court humour, born of the fancy, touched with softness, feeble-winged. Heart supplanted brain, and senses sense.

For all this Fletcher was to blame, or, if the causes were deeper, he stands a figurehead for our abuse. What the causes of such movements are, it is always difficult to say. The gradual change in the *personnel* of the theatre and its audiences may have had something to do with it. Puritanism and democracy were becoming gradually and deplorably identified. This meant that the theatre was being based on only one class. The audiences were becoming upper-class, or of the upper-class party; it is even more noteworthy that the same thing was happening to the dramatists. Henceforward they were almost entirely drawn from court circles and the upper classes. Or the reason for the degeneracy may have lain in some deeper weariness of men's hearts. Anyhow, the degeneracy was there. Splendour became softness and tragedy tragi-comedy. These later dramatists were like Ophelia.

"Thought and affliction, passion, hell itself,

She turns to favour and to prettiness."

It was in this sinking to prettiness and to absence of seriousness that the "degeneracy" of the later Elizabethan drama lies, not, as some modern critics say, in the selection of such admirable subjects as incest for their dramas. Compare a typical Fletcherian tragedy, *Bonduca*, with one of its predecessors. It is the absence of serious intention, the only desire to please, the lack of *artistic* morality, that make such plays, with their mild jokes, their co-ordinate double plots, and their unreality, so ultimately dreary and fifth-rate to a sensible reader. But such stuff overwhelmed England. That vulgarest of writers, Middleton, who had been doing admirable, coarse, low-level comedy, rather Jonsonian and quite realistic, turned about 1609 to romantic comedy. And by 1612 even Tourneur had written a tragi-comedy, *The Nobleman*.

But even when the triumph of prettiness was on its way to completion, there was one slightly old-fashioned figure still faithful to that larger prime. Serious tragedy seems only to have reached Webster, after it had left everybody else. In 1612 and 1613 he wrote two of the most amazing products of that amazing period. His powerful personality coloured what he wrote, and yet these two plays are more representative than any that had led to them, of the period behind them. The stream swept straight on from Marston and Tourneur to Webster. With him the sinister waves, if they lost something of their strange iridescence, won greater gloom and profundity. After him they plunged into the depths of earth. He stands in his loneliness, first of that long line of "last Elizabethans." As the edge of a cliff seems higher than the rest for the sheer descent in front of it, Webster, the Webster of these two plays, appears even mistier and grander than he really is, because he is the last of Earth, looking out over a sea of saccharine.

[1] *Das bürgerliche Trauerspiel in England.* Singer. The list counts *Arden of Feversham* as 1592. It is probably earlier, 1586 or so.

CHAPTER IV

JOHN WEBSTER

JOHN WEBSTER is one of the strangest figures in our literature. He was working for quite twenty years. We have at least four plays in which he collaborated, and three by him alone; but through all the period and in all his work he is quite ordinary and undistinguished, except for two plays which come quite close together in the middle. For two or three years, about 1612, he was a great genius; for the rest he was, if not indistinguishable, entirely commonplace. Coleridge does not more extraordinarily prove Apollonian fickleness. Webster makes one believe successful art depends as much on a wild chance, a multiple coincidence, as Browning found love did. If he had not had time in that middle period; if it had come a little later, under the Fletcherian influence; if he had been born twenty years later; if—... He was just in time; the subjects just suited him; the traditional atmosphere of the kind of play called out his greatest gifts; the right influence had preceded him; he was somehow not free to write the "true dramatic poem" or "sententious tragedy" he wanted to. And so these two great tragedies happened to exist. That easy and comfortable generalisation of the Philistine, "genius will out!" finds signal refutation in Webster. I shall give a short general account of his life and activities, and then examine his work more closely.

We know a great deal about Webster's life. He was born in the latter half of the sixteenth century, and died some time before the end of the seventeenth. He was an Elizabethan dramatist, a friend of Dekker and Chapman and Heywood. He was an odd genius who created slowly and borrowed a great deal. He was not very independent. . . .

It is, unimportantly, true that fewer "facts" than truths are known about him. We are luckily spared the exact dates of his uninteresting birth and death, and his unmeaning address and family. We have not even enough to serve as a framework for the elaborate structure of "doubtless" and "We may picture to ourselves young—" that stands as a biography of Shakespeare and others. It could, of course, be done by throwing our knowledge of Elizabethan conditions and our acquaintance with the character of the author of *The Duchess of Malfi* together. It would not be worth it. We know that Webster was a member of the Merchant Tailors' Company, and born free of it. There is a late legend that he was clerk of St Andrew's, Holborn. At one time it seemed possible to identify him (contemporary enemies tried to) with an ex-army chaplain who wrote fanatical religious tracts and was a University reformer, in the middle of the seventeenth century. Superb thought! It is hard to degenerate nobly; and his contemporaries, after reaching their summit, went down-hill (as writers) in various ways. Some became dropsical; others entered the Church; others went on writing; a few drank. But this, this would have been an end worthy of a fantastic poet! Alas! Mr Dyce investigated too thoroughly, and pretty certainly disproved the identification. After his last play, Webster slips from us inscrutably round the corner. He may have lived on for years and years. He may have died directly. It does not matter to us.

For the life of Webster the dramatist, however, as opposed to Webster the private man, we have a few facts. He comes into our notice—fairly young, it is to be presumed—in 1602. He was then very busily one of the less important of a band of hack playwrights employed by Henslowe. He had a hand in several plays that we know of during that year; *Cæsar's Fall, Two Shapes,*[1] *Christmas comes but once a year*, and at least one part of *Lady Jane*. His collaborators were Munday, Drayton, Middleton, Heywood, Chettle, Smith, and Dekker. It was the beginning, as far as we know, of a close connection with Dekker and a long one with Heywood. Webster was writing for both Henslowe's companies, *Cæsar's Fall* and *Two Shapes* for the Admiral's men, *Christmas comes but once a year* and *Lady Jane* for Worcester's men. Writing for Henslowe was not the best school for genius. No high artistic standard was exacted. It rather implies poverty, and certainly means scrappy and unserious work. It may have given Webster—it would have given some people—a sense of the theatre. But he emerged with so little facility in writing, and so little aptitude for a good plot (in the ordinary sense), that one must conclude that his genius was not best fitted for theatrical expression, into which it was driven. There are other periods and literary occupations it is harder to imagine him in. But I can figure him as a more or less realistic novelist of the present or the last eighty years, preferably from Russia. His literary skill, his amazing genius for incorporating fragments of his experience, his "bitter flashes" and slow brooding atmosphere of gloom, would have been more tremendous untrammelled by dramatic needs. His power of imaginative visualisation was often superfluous in a play. Like most of his gifts it is literary. It is just what one keenly misses in most novels. One can see, almost quote from, a rather large grey-brown novel by John Webster, a book full of darkly suffering human beings, slightly less inexplicable than Dostoieffsky's, but as thrilling, figures glimpsed by sudden flashes that tore the gloom they were part of; a book such that one would remember the taste of the whole longer than any incident or character. . . . But these imaginations are foolish in an Heraclitan world, and the phrase "John Webster in the nineteenth century" has no meaning.

Webster seems to have had the ordinary training, collaborating in classical tragedy, history, and low comedy. None of his collaborators left much mark on his style. He was more subservient than impressionable. The only play of this lot that we have is *Lady Jane*, printed in a cut form as *Sir Thomas Wyatt*. Webster probably had a good deal to do with two Scenes, 2 and 16;[1] he may be responsible for more, but, if so, it is indistinguishable. The whole play is a ramshackle, primitive (for 1602), ordinary affair. The parts we think Webster's are rather different from the rest, but no better. Metrically they are hopeless, but that may be due to the state of the play. There is a sort of sleepy imagination in—

"Lo, we ascend into our chairs of state,
Like funeral coffins, in some funeral pomp,
Descending to their graves!"

It gratifies one with a feeling of fitness, that Webster should have been thinking of funerals so early as this. Perhaps one is sentimentally misled, and it is really someone else's work. The whole thing is equally uncertain and unimportant.

The Induction to *The Malcontent* (1604), our earliest example of Webster's unaided writing, is a slight piece of work, and valueless. The stiff involved sentences are characteristic. The humour is commonplace. It all shows up dully by the rest of the play, which is restive and inflamed with the vigorous, queer, vital, biting style of Marston.

Webster seems to have gone on in the profession of a hack author. He must have collaborated in dozens of plays in these years, perhaps written some of his own. He next comes to light writing two comedies of London life with Dekker, *Westward Ho* (1604) and *Northward Ho* (1605). This time it is good work he is concerned with, though out of his true line. They were written for the Children of Paul's. Webster seems to have been a free-lance at this period, going from company to company. But he must somehow have got a sort of reputation by this time, to be joined with Dekker in this friendly skirmish against Chapman, Jonson, and Marston (*Eastward Ho*), who were all eminent. And in 1607 it seems to have been worth a publisher's while to put his and Dekker's names on the title-page of *Sir Thomas Wyatt*, and leave out Chettle, Smith, and Heywood. In *Westward Ho* and *Northward Ho* there are a few scenes I think we can be pretty certain are mainly Webster's; *Northward Ho*, II. 2. and V. 1, very probably *Westward Ho*, I.1. and III. 3, and quite probably *Northward Ho*, I. 1. and III. 1. One seems to catch a sight of him elsewhere in the plays; but it is difficult to be certain. In the scenes we attribute to him, the sound of a deeper, graver, and duller voice than Dekker's seems to be heard. It is not altogether fancy. The lightness goes. The bawdy jokes change their complexion a little; they come more from the heart and less from the pen. The people in the play do not live any the more or the less, but they become more like dead men and less like lively dolls. The whole thing grows less dramatic; the characters become self-consciously expository—Webster was always old-fashioned in this—instead of talking to each other, half-face to us, they turn towards the audience and stand side by side, addressing it. Justiniano's jealousy grows more serious and real when Webster takes charge of him, more unpleasantly real to himself, and fantastically expressed. And (*Northward Ho*, II. 2) Mistress Mayberry's sudden disappearance to cry stirs you with an unexpected little stab of pathetic reality not unlike the emotion the later Webster can arouse when he will. But the whole outlines and atmosphere of the plays, and the characters and incidents, are far nearer Dekker than Webster. It is only possible to say either that Webster was merely assisting Dekker in these plays, or that his peculiar individuality was either ungrown or dormant. No doubt his romantic classical ideas made him feel he was writing very far down to the public. But he need not have been ashamed, and it may very well have done him good. Good farce is a worthy training for a tragic writer; and these plays are excellent comic farce. The wit is not subtle, the plots have no psychological interest, and the ragging of Chapman is primitive. But the characters have a wealth of vitality, spirits, and comic value. The jokes are often quite good, especially the bawdy ones, and the sequence of events keeps your mind lively and attentive. The general atmosphere in these two plays has a tang of delightful, coarse gaiety, like a country smell in March. They are really quite good, for the rough knock-about stuff they are; among the best in their kind, and that no bad kind. It would be amusing, if it were not so irritating, that many who are authorities in Elizabethan literature are violently and angrily shocked by these two plays, and condemn them as filth. Dr Ward throws up hands of outraged refinement. Professor Schelling has an incredibly funny passage. "They mark the depth of gross and vicious realism to which the comedy of manners descended. . . . Some of the figures we would fain believe, in their pruriency and outspoken uncleanliness of speech, represent an occasional aberration, if not an outrageous exaggeration, of the manners of the time. . . . In our admiration of the ideal heights at times attained by the literature of the great age of Elizabeth we are apt to forget that the very amplitude of its vibrations involves an extraordinary range, and that we must expect depths and morasses as well as wholesome and bracing moral heights. . . ." If literary criticism crosses Lethe, and we could hear the comments of the foul-mouthed ghosts of Shakespeare, Marlowe, and Webster on this too common attitude, their outspoken uncleanliness would prostrate Professor Schelling and his friends. Anger at this impudent attempt to thrust the filthy and degraded standards of the modern middle-class drawing-room on the clean fineness of the Elizabethans, might be irrelevant in an Essay of this sort. What is relevant is a protest that such thin-lipped writers are not only ridiculous on this point, but also, for all their learning and patience, without sufficient authority in Elizabethan literature. It is impossible to trust them. Even in deciding a date, it may be necessary to have sympathy with the Elizabethans. The Elizabethans liked obscenity; and the primness and the wickedness that do not like it, have no business with them.

There is a silence of some six years after *Northward Ho*. We do not know what Webster was doing. Somehow he was gaining position, and preparing himself. In 1611 or 1612 he produced *The White Devil*, the first of the two plays which definitely and uniquely give the world Webster. Last heard of he was a subordinate collaborator; now he is a great, very individual dramatist. The step was enormous; but he had a long time to make it in. If Fate had spared us some of his interim works, we might not be so surprised.

The preface to *The White Devil* is important for the light it throws both on Webster and on the general critical ideas of the period. "Evidemment," says M. Symmes, "Webster dans ce passage est un des premiers à con-naitre l'importance, le mérite, et l'individualité du théâtre anglais romantique, commegenre séparé."[1] It is too strong. But he does seem to hover in a queer way, between intense pride in his own work and fine appreciation of the best among his contemporaries, and scorn of all these in comparison to a "true dramatic poem" in the classical style. He shows himself wholly of the Jonson-Chapman school of classicists, in agreement with the more cultivated critics. His gloom fires up at the imaginary glories of these Saturnian plays; he is superb in his scorn of his own audience. "Should a man present to such an auditory the most sententious tragedy that ever was written, observing all the critical laws, as height of style, and gravity of person, enrich it with the sententious Chorus, and, as it were, life in death in the passionate and weighty Nuntius; . . ." His arrogance was partly due, no doubt, to pique at the failure of the play and partly to the literary fashion. But it had something natural to him. Even in these plays he so scornfully wrote for the "uncapable multitude" of those times there is a sort of classicism. His temperament was far too romantic for it; he was not apt to it, like Chapman. Yet, especially in *The White Devil*, the unceasing couplets at the end of speeches, both in their number and their nature, have a curious archaic effect. One line is connected with the situation, and expresses an aspect of it; the next, with the pat expected rhyme, goes to the general rule, and turns the moral. It belonged to Webster's ideal temperament in poetry to turn readily and continually to the greater generalisations. These last lines or couplets always lead out on to them. They went, the classicists, with a kind of glee; they liked to be in touch with permanent vaguenesses.

Webster's praise of his contemporaries is, however, very discriminating. The order he gives them is instructive:— Chapman; Jonson; Beaumont and Fletcher; Shakespeare, Dekker, and Heywood. He tells us in this preface, what we could have guessed, that he wrote very slowly. It was natural, as he compiled, rather than composed, his plays; working so laboriously from his notebook. He may be imagined following doggedly behind inspiration, glooming over a situation till he saw the heart of it in a gesture or a phrase. He casts the sigh of the confirmed constipate at Heywood and Dekker and Shakespeare for their "right happy and copious industry." His agonies in composition are amusingly described in a passage in Fitzjeffry's *Notes from Blackfriars* (1620).[1]

The White Devil and *The Duchess of Malfi* are often described as "revenge-plays," a recently-invented genus. Dr. Stoll deals at great length with them in this light, and

Professor Vaughan devotes two or three pages of his short essay to summing up the history of the type. There is something in the idea, but not much; and it has been over-worked. To begin with, there are far fewer examples of this type than these critics believe. And it is not quite clear what is the thread of continuity they are thinking of. Is it the fact that revenge is the motive in each play? Or is it a special type of play, the criterion of which is its atmosphere, and which generally includes vengeance as a motive? If the second, they must include other plays in their list; if the first, drop some out. The truth is that there is a certain type of play, the plot of which was based on blood-for-blood vendetta, and the atmosphere of which had a peculiar tinge. Kyd started it; it dropped for a bit, and then Marston revived it, rather differently, with great foresight, at an opportune moment. It had a brief boom with Marston, Shakespeare, and Chettle. The atmosphere became indistinguishable from that of a good many plays of the period. Tourneur took the atmosphere, and discarded the revenge-plot, in *The Atheist's Tragedy*. So did *The Second Maiden's Tragedy*. Chapman happened to take the revenge-motive, and went back to Seneca on his own account. He gives a characteristic account of the metaphysics of the revenge-motive in the *Revenge of Bussy*.[1] Webster used it a little in one of two plays that in other ways resemble the work of other people who used the revenge-plot. That is all. To call *The Duchess of Malfi* a revenge-play is simply ridiculous. If it is raked in, you must include *Othello* and a dozen more as well. The whole category is a false one. It would be much more sensible to invent and trace the "Trial-at-law" type, beginning with the *Eumenides*, going down through *The Merchant of Venice, The White Devil, Volpone, The Spanish Curate*, and a score more, till you ended with *Justice*.

The White Devil and *the Duchess of Malfi* are so similar in atmosphere that it is sometimes difficult for the moment to remember in which of them some character or speech occurs. But it is convenient to consider them separately; and to take *The White Devil* first.

The story is simple. Brachiano conceives a passion for Vittoria, and wins her. She suggests, and he plans, the death of Camillo and Isabella. Their love is discovered by Vittoria's mother, Cornelia. Isabella's brothers, Francisco and Monticelso, try to put an end to it, by giving it rope to hang itself. Before this plan can take effect the murders are committed. Francisco and Monticelso arraign Vittoria for complicity in the murders and for adultery. She is condemned to imprisonment; but Francisco, to bring the two nearer final ruin, plots so that she and Brachiano escape together to Padua and marry. Thither he follows them, with some friends, in disguise; and accomplishes their deaths.

Webster did not handle this tale very skilfully, from the dramaturgic point of view. The play is almost a dramatised narrative. Occasionally the clumsiness of his hand is uncomfortably manifest. Generally it does not matter, for his virtues lie in a different aspect of plays from plot-making. The motives of the various characters are more obscure than they are wont to be in Elizabethan plays. On the whole this is a virtue; or seems to be to the modern mind. Characters in a play gain in realism and a mysterious solemnity, if they act unexplainedly on instinct, like people in real life, and not on rational and publicly-stated grounds, like men in some modern plays.

The play begins with a bang. From the point of view of the plot it is an unusual and unhelpful beginning. Count Lodovico (who turns out later in the play to be an unsuccessful lover of Isabella, and who becomes the chief instrument in the downfall of Brachiano and Vittoria) has just been banished. He enters with a furious shout. "Banished!" In this scene there is an instance of a favourite dramatic trick of Webster's, to add liveliness. When some long speech has to be made, where Chapman would give it to one person, Webster divides it between two, continually alternating with a few lines each. It makes the scene "go" in a most remarkable manner. In this case Gasparo and Antonelli do it to Lodovico. In *The Duchess oj Malfi* Ferdinand and the

Cardinal treat the Duchess in this way.

The next scene introduces the chief characters and the chief emotion. This fatal love, the cause of the whole tragedy, enters most strikingly. Vittoria leaves the stage, Brachiano turns, with a flaming whisper, to Flamineo. He wastes no words. He does not foolishly tell the audience, "I am in love with that woman who has just gone off."

BRACHIANO. "Flamineo——"

FLAMINEO. "My lord?"

BRACHIANO. "Quite lost, Flamineo."

Webster thought dramatically.

Flamineo, a typical knave of Webster's, fills the next few pages with a chorus of quotations from Montaigne. Dramatic is the juxtaposition of the passionate scene between Brachiano and Vittoria, broken by the prophetic Cornelia, the baiting of Brachiano by the Duke and the Cardinal, and the pitiful interview of Brachiano and his deserted wife. In the last Webster shews that he can turn to more untroubled tragedy when he wants to:

"I pray sir, burst my heart; and in my death

Turn to your ancient pity, though not love."

Rather swiftly, Vittoria (perhaps) and Brachiano, certainly, accomplish the murders; and Vittoria is arrested and tried. The trial scene is prodigiously spirited. There is no hero to enlist our sympathy; it is merely a contest between various unquenchable wickednesses. The rattle of rapid question and answer, sharp with bitterness, is like musketry. Vittoria is wicked; but her enemies are wicked and mean. So one sides with her, and even admires. Her spirit of ceaseless resistance and fury, like the wriggling of a trapped cat, is astonishing.

"For your names
Of whore and murdress, they proceed from you,
As if a man should spit against the wind;
The filth returns in's face."

Flamineo's subsequent affectation of madness and melancholy is made too much of; for the purpose of amusing, perhaps. At this point in the play, the two "villains" part company. Francisco pursues his way alone. The scene between Brachiano, in his groundless jealousy, and Vittoria, is tremendous with every kind of beauty and horror; beginning from the extraordinarily un-Websterian:

"How long have I beheld the devil in crystal!
Thou hast led me, like an heathen sacrifice,
With music and with fatal yokes of flowers,
To my eternal ruin. Woman to man
Is either a god or a wolf."

The taming of the wild cat, Vittoria, is shown with wonderfully precise and profound psychology; and all made horrible by the ceaseless and eager prompting of Flamineo.

"Fie, fie, my lord!

Women are caught as you take tortoises;
She must be turned on her back."

The scene of the election of the Pope is an irrelevant ornament. It is noteworthy that to some extent Webster improved in dramatic craft with time. *The Duchess of Malfi* has fewer such scenes than *The White Devil*.

The last part of the play, after it removes to Padua, is one long study of the horror of death. It takes it from every point of view. There is the pathetic incomprehension of Cornelia over young Marcello. "Alas 1 he is not dead; he is in a trance. Why, here's nobody shall get anything by his death. Let me call him again for God's sake."

There is the difficulty and struggle of the death of so intensely live a man as Brachiano:

"Oh, thou strong heart!
There's such a covenant 'tween the world and it,
They're loath to break."

There is the grotesque parody of death, in Flamineo's

"Oh I smell soot,
Most stinking soot! The chimney is afire. . . .
There's a plumber laying pipes in my guts, it scalds."

There is the superbness of Vittoria's courage;

"Yes I shall welcome death
As princes do some great ambassadors;
I'll meet thy weapon half-way."

There are the "black storm" and the "mist" which drive around Vittoria and Flamineo in the last moments of all.

The Duchess of Malfi is on the whole a better play than *The White Devil*. It does not have more of Webster's supreme dramatic moments, but the language is more rich and variously moving—in a dramatic, not merely a literary way. It is, even more than *The White Devil*, in the first half a mere simple narrative of events, leading up to a long-continued and various hell in the second part. It is often discussed if the plots of *The White Devil* and *The Duchess of Malfi* are weak. Webster's method does not really take cognisance of a plot in the ordinary sense of the word. He is too atmospheric. It is like enquiring if there is bad drawing in a nocturne of Whistler's.

The Duchess of Malfi is a young widow, forbidden by her brothers, Ferdinand and the Cardinal, to marry again. They put a creature of theirs, Bosola, into her service as a spy. The Duchess loves and secretly marries her steward, Antonio, and has three children. Bosola ultimately discovers and reports this. Antonio and the Duchess have to fly. The Duchess is captured, imprisoned, and mentally tortured and put to death. Ferdinand goes mad. In the last Act he, the Cardinal, Antonio, and Bosola are all killed with various confusions and in various horror.

The play begins more slowly than *The White Devil*. Bosola

appears near the beginning, and plays throughout a part like that of Flamineo. The great scene in the first Act is the scene of the Duchess's proposal to Antonio. It is full of that perfect, tender beauty which the stormy Webster could evoke when he liked; from the Duchess's preliminary farewell to her maid,

Good dear soul,
Wish me good speed;
For I am going into a wilderness
Where I shall find nor path nor friendly clue
To be my guide."

to the maid's concluding comment:

"Whether the spirit of greatness or of woman
Reign most in her, I know not; but it shows
A fearful madness: I owe her much of pity."

There is rather hideous and very typical tragedy in the scene of Bosola's device to discover the Duchess's secret. The meeting of Bosola and Antonio, at midnight, after the birth of the child, is full of dramatic power and of breathless suspense that worthily recalls *Macbeth*.

ANT. "Bosola! . . .
heard you not
A noise even now?
BOS. From whence?
ANT. From the Duchess's lodging.

BOS. Not I: did you?

ANT. I did, or else I dreamed.

BOS. Let's walk towards it.

ANT. No: it may be 'twas

But the rising of the wind.

BOS. Very likely. . . ."

When the news is brought to the brothers that the Duchess has had a child, their anger is hideous and, as with passionate people, too imaginative.

After this, and before the events which lead to the catastrophe, that is, between the second and third Acts, there is a long and somewhat clumsy interval. This was rather in the dramatic fashion of the time. Ferdinand's discovery of the Duchess's guilt breaks finely across a lovely scene of domestic merriment. The plot unravels swiftly. The final parting of the Duchess and Antonio is full of a remarkable quiet beauty of phrase and poetry. It is a mere accident that we have discovered that it is entirely composed of fragments of, and adaptations from, Sidney, Donne, Ben Jonson, and others. The scenes of the various tortures of the Duchess form an immense and not always successful symphony of gloom, horror, madness, and death. It is only redeemed by the fact that the Duchess can never be quite broken:

"I am Duchess of Malfi still."

Only once, just before death, does she let an hysterical cry escape her:

"any way, for Heaven's sake,

So I were out of your whispering."

The superhuman death of the Duchess is finely anti-climaxed by the too human death of Cariola, who fights, kicks, prays, and lies.

After the death of the Duchess, there is a slight lull before the rest of the tragedy rises again to its climax. It contains a queer scene of *macabre* comedy where Ferdinand beats his fantastic doctor, and a curious, rather Gothic, extraneous scene of quietness, where Antonio talks to the echo. The end is a maze of death and madness. Webster's supreme gift is the blinding revelation of some intense state of mind at a crisis, by some God-given phrase. All the last half of *The Duchess of Malfi* is full of them. The mad Ferdinand, stealing across the stage in the dark, whispering to himself, with the devastating impersonality of the madman, "Strangling is a very quiet death," is a figure one may not forget. And so in the next scene, the too sane Cardinal:—

"How tedious is a guilty conscience!

When I look into the fish-ponds in my garden

Methinks I see a thing armed with a rake

That seems to strike at me."

It is one of those pieces of imagination one cannot explain, only admire.

But it is, of course, in or near the moment of death that Webster is most triumphant. He adopts the romantic convention, that men are, in the second of death, most essentially and significantly themselves. In the earlier play the whole angry, sickening fear of death that a man feels who has feared nothing else, lies in those terrific words of Brachiano's, when it comes home to him that he is fatally poisoned:—

"On pain of death, let no man name death to me:
It is a word infinitely terrible."

Webster knows all the ways of approaching death. Flamineo, with the strange carelessness of the dying man, grows suddenly noble. "What dost think on?" his murderer asks him.

FLAMINEO. "Nothing; of nothing: leave thy idle questions.

I am i' the way to study a long silence:
To prate were idle. I remember nothing.
There's nothing of so infinite vexation
As man's own thoughts."

And Webster, more than any man in the world, has caught the soul just in the second of its decomposition in death, when knowledge seems transcended, and the darkness closes in, and boundaries fall away.

"My soul," cries Vittoria, "like to a ship in a black storm,

Is driven, I know not whither."

And Flamineo—

"While we look up to Heaven we confound

Knowledge with knowledge, O, I am in a mist."

So in this play Ferdinand "seems to come to himself," as Bosola says, "now he's so near the bottom." He is still half-mad; but something of the old overweening claim, on the universe fires up in the demented brain:

"Give me some wet hay: I am broken-minded.

I do account this world but a dog-kennel:

I will vault credit and affect high pleasures

Beyond death."

For some six years again, after *The Duchess of Malfi*, we know nothing of Webster's activities. When he comes once more into sight, in *The Devil's Law-Case* (1620) he has shared the fate of the whole drama. It is an attempt to write in the Massinger-Fletcher genus of tragi-comedy. The plot is of so complicated a nature that it would take almost the space of the whole play to set it out fully. Indeed there is scarcely a plot at all, but a succession of plots, interwoven, and each used, in the debased way of that period, almost only to produce some ingeniously startling scene, some theatrical paradox. It was, probably, Fletcher who was responsible for this love of a succession of dramatic shocks. It suited a part of Webster's taste only too well.

The main incident of the play is a malicious suit brought by a mother, Leonora, against her son, Romelio, trying to dispossess him on the (false) ground of bastardy. Tacked on to that are various minor affairs, a duel between friends in which both are supposed to have been killed and both marvellously survive, a virgin pretending to be with child, a sick man miraculously cured by an assassin's unintentionally medicinal knife, and so on. The most central incident may have been suggested to Webster by an old play, *Lust's Dominion*; the cure he got from a translation of some French yarns. But the question of his originality is unimportant. All his incidents aim at that cheap fantasticality which marked this Jacobean drama. And his topics are its well-rubbed coins, romantic friendship, sudden "passion," virginity, duelling, seduction. A most dully debonair world. However, he could not handle them with the same touch. Webster stepped the same measures as his contemporaries, willingly enough— conceitedly even, as his dedication and preface show; but with earlier legs. His characters alternate between being the sometimes charming lay-figures of the time, and wakening to the boisterous liveliness of fifteen years before. Several scenes are very noticeably Jonsonian interludes of farce, sandwiched between comedy. The vigorous flow of Act II, Scene 1 (pages 114-116) is wholly reminiscent of the comedy of humours. This is partly due to the purely satiric character of some of the passages. The dramatists of the beginning of the century loved to play Juvenal. They would still be railing. Webster was especially prone to it. Repeatedly, in the *Devil's Law-Case*, this habit of abuse, directed against one person or the world, recalls Webster's two great plays. There are a score of passages where you immediately cry "Webster!" the note is so individual. And they are mostly of this satiric kind. Who else could have written (I. 1):

"With what a compell'd face a woman sits
While she is drawing! I have noted divers,
Either to feign smiles, or suck in the lips,
To have a little mouth; ruffle the cheeks
To have the dimple seen; and so disorder
The face with affectation, at next sitting
It has not been the same: . . ."

The "I have noted" of the professional satirist is unmistakeable.

But, indeed, the essence of Webster pervades this "tragi-comedy." And the result is that it is as far different from other tragi-comedies in its spirit, as *Measure for Measure* is from the comedies among which it is numbered. His vocabulary and peculiar use of words peep out on every page; "passionately," "infinitely," "screech-owl," "a lordship," "caroche," "mathematical," "dunghill," "foul" a hundred times; and all in sentences that have the very run of his accents. There are scores of short passages. Webster's characters have the trick of commenting on themselves when they are jesting. "You see my lord, we are merry." cries Romelio (p. 111), and so Sanitonella (p. 114), "I am merry." The Duchess inevitably comes to one's mind, in that happy moment before her world crumbled about her, "I prithee, when were we so merry?" It is a trick that makes the transience or the unreality of their merriment stand out against the normal and real gloom. Continually in this play, as in the others, Webster is referring to women painting their faces. The subject had a queer fascination for him. Those other, more obvious, thoughts of his reappear, too; his broodings on death and graves. There is the same savagery in his mirth:

"But do you not think"

says Jolenta, suddenly, when she has acceded to Romelio's horrible plannings.

"I shall have a horrible strong breath now?"

ROMELIO. "Why?"

JOLENTA. "O, with keeping your counsel, 'tis so terrible foul."

"Bitter flashes" Romelio rightly calls such outbursts. But he himself achieves wit most successfully in the same mood and manner. When the Capuchin worries him, before his duel, about religion, he, "very melancholy," retorts with a question about swords—

"These things, you know," the Capuchin replies, "are out of my practice."

"But these are things, you know,
I must practise with to-morrow."

Romelio sardonically returns. It is very clear throughout that the bitterer Webster's flashes are, the brighter. And in a similar way he livens up when he approaches any emotion such as Jolenta describes, in herself, as "fantastical sorrow." It is the fantastical in emotion or character that inspires him, while the fantastical in situation leaves him comparatively cold. He essays the latter, dutifully—the usual intellectual paradoxes and morbid conventions of impossible psychology which this kind of drama demanded. In that typically-set Websterian scene (Act III. Scene 3—*A table set forth with two tapers, a death's-head, a book.*) between Romelio and Jolenta, love, hate, passion, anger, and grief play General Post with all the unnatural speed the Jacobeans loved. He has even invested the starts and turns of the trial-scene with a good deal of interest and much dramatic power. But the anguish that apes mirth and the mirth that toys with pain wake his genius. He even laughs at himself. You feel an almost personal resentment at being sold, towards the end of the play. Romelio's sullen but impressive stoicism is broken by Leonora's entrance with coffins and winding-sheets and that incomparable dirge.

"... Courts adieu, and all delights,
　All bewitching appetites!
　Sweetest breath and clearest eye,
　like perfumes, go out and die;
　And consequently this is done
　As shadows wait upon the sun.
　Vain the ambition of kings,
　Who seek by trophies and dead things
　To leave a living name behind,
　And weave but nets to catch the wind."

Romelio, like any reader, is caught by the utter beauty of this. He melts in repentance, persuades his mother, and then the priest, to enter the closet, and then—locks them in with entire callousness and a dirty jest, and goes off to his duel. It is, literally, shocking. But Romelio is one of the two or three characters into whom Webster has breathed a spasmodic life and force. The ordinary dolls of the drama, like Contarino and Ercole, remain dolls in his hands. But the lust and grief of Leonora have some semblance of motion, the suffering of Jolenta has an hysterical truth, and the figure of Romelio lives sometimes with the vitality of an intruder from another world. He comes out of the earlier drama. He is largely the sort of monster Ben Jonson or Marlowe, or Kyd or Tourneur, or the earlier Webster likes to picture, malign, immoral, grotesque, and hideously alive. Winifred also is older than 1620. She has an unpleasant vivacity, a rank itch of vulgarity, as well as the office of commentator, which reminds one of characters in Webster's two great plays. She is a Bosola in skirts. A sure sign, she grows more excited when love-making is to hand. It is typical of Webster that he should smirch with his especial rankness, not only the baser characters of this play, but the love-making between his hero and heroine, as he does through Winifred's mouth in the second scene of the play. like any Flamineo, she interprets between us and the puppets' dallying, a little disgustingly:

"O sweet-breath'd monkeys, how they grow together!" . . .

A few incidents stand out, marked by the darker range of colours of the earlier drama. Contarino's groan that announces that he is not dead (III. 2):

CON. "O!"

FIRST SURGEON. "Did he not groan?"

SECOND SURGEON. "Is the wind in that door still?"

has something of the terror and abrupt ghostliness of the midnight scene in *The Duchess of Malfi* (II. 3), or *Macbeth*, or Jonson's additions to *The Spanish Tragedy*. And Leonora's mad flinging herself on the ground in III. 3, and lying there, is an old trick that the early Elizabethan audiences almost demanded as an essential of Tragedy. It goes back through Ferdinand, Bussy, and Marston's heroes, to old Hieronimo himself.

Webster's note-book is perhaps a little less apparent in this play than in the two previous. But there are a good many passages we can identify, and a lot more we can suspect. He had fewer "meditations" of the old railing order to compile from his pages of aphorisms and modern instances. But we find repetitions from *A Monumental Column, The White Devil*, and especially *The Duchess of Malfi*; and Ben Jonson and Sidney have found their way through the note-book into these pages. He still employs soliloquy and the concluding couplet to an extent and in a way that seem queer in a play of this period. But he seems to have become a little more sensible to violent incongruity. He never offends so harshly as he had used. Occasionally, still, the stage-machinery creaks loudly enough to disturb the theatrical illusion rather unpleasantly. Sanitonella is a little abrupt and blunt in exacting information from Crispiano for our benefit:—"But, pray, sir, resolve me, what should be the reason that you . . ." etc. (II. 1). And Romelio's asides are occasionally rather too obvious. In III. 3, when his various proposals to Jolenta have been ineffectual, he is non-plussed; but only for a second:

ROMELIO (*aside*)   "This will not do.

The devil has on the sudden furnished me
With a rare charm, yet a most unnatural
Falsehood: no matter, so 'twill take.—"

But at the end, when everybody reveals who he is, and begins explaining everything that has happened, the tedium of these disentanglings is cut, and the apparently inevitable boredom dodged, by a device that is so audacious in its simplicity as to demand admiration. Leonora, who has apparently made good use of her imprisonment in the closet to jot down a *précis* of all the plots in the play, interrupts the growing flood of explanations with

"Cease here all further scrutiny. This paper
    Shall give unto the court each circumstance
    Of all these passages!"

One is too relieved to object.

Metrically this play is very similar to its two forerunners; though here, as in the handling, Webster seems a little quieter. He is unaffected by the Fletcher influence in metre. The run of his lines is still elusive and without any marked melody, except in one or two passages. The beginning lines with the continual shifting and sliding of accent, and the jerky effect of conversation, continue. It was always a blank verse for talking rather than reading. One trick Webster seems to have developed further, the filling out of feet with almost inadequate syllables. Twice in the first five pages "marriage" is a trisyllable. "Emotion" fills two feet; and so on. This habit, common between 1580 and 1595, was revived by some writers after 1615. It fits in very queerly with that opposite tendency to the use of trisyllabic feet that Webster greatly indulged in. Sometimes the combination is rather piquant. But "marriage" is, perhaps, a symptom of an increased steadiness and mastery of rhythm. There are two or three passages where his blank verse is abler and better, in considerable periods, not in short fragments and exclamations, than it had been before. And this is accompanied by a greater evenness. Leonora's great speech (III. 8) begins with something of the old ripple: but it dies away:

". . . Is he gone then?
There is no plague i' the world can be compared
To impossible desire; for they are plagu'd
In the desire itself. . . .
O, I shall run mad!
For as we love our youngest children best,
So the last fruit of our affection,
Where-ever we bestow it, is most strong,
Most violent, most unresistable,
Since 'tis indeed our latest harvest-home,
Last merriment 'fore winter. . . ."

The beauty and pathos of these lines, the complete and masterful welding of music and meaning, show what fineness is in *The Devil's Law-Case.* One could quote many other things as noble, or as admirable, from Romelio's glorious

"I cannot set myself so many fathom
Beneath the height of my true heart, as fear,"

or the sagacious and horrid rightness of his

"doves never couple without
A kind of murmur,"

to Jolenta's cry,

"O, if there be another world i' the moon
As some fantastics dream. . . ."

Yet the play is not a good play. These good bits illuminate, for the most part, nothing but themselves, and have only a literary value. A good play must leave an increasing impression of beauty or terror or mirth upon the mind, heaping its effect continually with a thousand trifles. This does not so. It is a play without wholeness. Its merits are occasional and accidental. If you read closely, there is the extraordinary personality of Webster plain enough over and in it all. But he was working in an uncongenial medium. It is a supreme instance of the importance of the right form to the artist. The Fletcher-Massinger "tragi-comedy" was the product of an age and temper as unsuitable to Webster as the tragedy of blood and dirt had been suitable. *The Devil's Law-Case* is not even a fine failure, as, for instance, *Timon of Athens* is. In the first place a tragicomedy is not a thing to make a fine failure of. And in the second place Webster's nature and methods demanded success in a right form, or nothing. He had to suffuse the play with himself. He was not great enough and romantic enough to confer immortality upon fragments. His bitter flashes required the background of thunderous darkness to show them up; against this grey daylight they are ineffectual.

Beyond the uninteresting and unimportant *A Monumental Column* (1613), which only shows how naturally Webster turned to the imitation of Donne when he turned to poetry, the uncertain and featureless *Monuments of Honour*, and a few rather perfunctory verses of commendation, we have nothing more of Webster's except *A Cure for a Cuckold*. This must have been written shortly after *The Devil's Law-Case*. It is almost entirely unimportant for throwing light on the real Webster. All we know is that he had something to do with the play; how much or little it is impossible to tell from reading it. He may be responsible for the whole of the main plot. That it is not so obscure and unmotivated as has sometimes been supposed, I have shown in an Appendix; but it is not good. Parts have a slight, unreal, charm for those who are interested in antiquities. The way in which in IV. 3 (p. 310) Lessingham suddenly sulks, and goes off to make mischief, in order to spin the play out for another act and a bit, is childish.

It is a pity we cannot barter with oblivion and give *A Cure for a Cuckold* for Ford and Webster's lost murder play.

This was one of the last, and it must have been one of the best, of the Elizabethan domestic tragedies. What a superb combination, Ford and Webster! And on such a subject! It may have been again, after all those years, the last cry of the true voice of Elizabethan drama. Once, in 1624, there was, perhaps, a tragedy of blood, not of sawdust. It is beyond our reach.

[1] Perhaps the same play. See Appendix B.

[1] Sc. 2 is from p. 186, col. 1, "*Enter* Guildford," to p. 187, " 'cave.' *Exeunt.*"

Sc. 16 is from p. 199, end, "*Enter* Winchester," to p. 201, " 'dumb' *Exeunt.*"

[1] Symmes: *Les Débute de la Critique Dramatique en Angleterre*, etc.

[1] Given in Dyce's 1857 edition. Introduction, p. xvl.

[1] Chapman's *Tragedies*, ed. Parrott, pp. 131-2.

CHAPTER V

SOME CHARACTERISTICS OF WEBSTER

IT happens, with some writers, that when you come to examine their less-known works, your idea of them suffers considerable change, and you realise that the common conception of them is incomplete, distorted, or even entirely wrong. This is not the case with Webster. He is known to everyone by two plays—*The Duchess of Malfi* and *The White Devil*. The most diligent study of the rest of his authentic works will scarcely add anything of value to that knowledge of him. He is a remarkable dramatist, with an unusually individual style and emotional view of the world. What "Webster," the literary personality, means to us, its precise character, and its importance, can be discovered and explained from these two plays. So I shall chiefly consider and quote them, with an occasional sidelight from *The Devil's Law-Case*.

It is one task of a critic, no doubt, to communicate exactly his emotions at what he is criticising, to express and define the precise savour. But it is not a thing one can go on at for long. Having tried to hint once or twice what "Webster" precisely is, I had better analyse various aspects of him, and not tiresomely, like some political speaker, seek about for a great many ways of saying the same thing. And after all, Webster carries his own sense and savour. A showman, "motley on back and pointing-pole in hand," can but draw attention, and deliver a prologue. If I can explain briefly to anyone the sort of plays Webster was writing, the sort of characters that he took delight in, the kind of verse he used, the kind of literary effect he probably aimed at—as I see all these things—I can then only take him up to a speech of the Duchess and leave him there. One cannot explain

"What would it pleasure me to have my throat cut
        With diamonds? or to be smothered
        With cassia? or to be shot to death with pearls?
        I know death hath ten thousand several doors
        For men to take their exits; and 'tis found
        They go on such strange geometrical hinges
        You may open them both ways: . . ."

To paraphrase it, or to hang it with epithets, would be silly, almost indecent. One can only quote. And though quotation is pleasant, it is a cheap way of filling space; and I have written this essay on the assumption that its readers will be able to have at least *The Duchess of Malfi* and *The White Devil* before them.

So I shall only attempt, in this chapter, to mention some of Webster's most interesting characteristics, and to analyse one or two of them.

His general position, as the rearguard of the great period in Elizabethan drama and literature, I have already outlined. He took a certain kind of play, a play with a certain atmosphere, which appealed to him, and made two works of individual genius. Beyond this type of play and the tradition of it, there are no very important "influences" on him. Shakespeare's studies of madness may have affected him. The Duchess,

> "I'll tell thee a miracle;
>> I am not mad yet, to my cause of sorrow;
>> The heaven o'er my head seems made of molten brass,
>> The earth of flaming sulphur, yet I am not mad,"

has a note of Lear in it, but also, and perhaps more definitely, of *Antonio and Mellida*. From Ben Jonson and Chapman he borrowed. And something of their attitude to drama became his. But he does not imitate them in any important individual quality. He pillaged Donne, too, as much of him as was accessible to a middle-class dramatist, and occasionally seems to emulate the extraordinary processes of that mind. The characters in Webster's plays, like the treatment of the story, in as far as they are not his own, are the usual characters of the drama of eight years before. Once only does he noticeably seem to take a figure from the popular gallery of the years in which he was writing. The little prince Giovanni, like Shakespeare's Mamillius, is adopted from the Beaumont and Fletcher children. He has the same precocity in wit (it seems a little distressing to modern taste), and more of their sentimentality than Hermione's son. But, against that background, he is, on the whole, a touching and lovely figure.

The one influence upon Webster that is always noticeable is that of satire. His nature tended to the outlook of satire; and his plays give evidence that he read Elizabethan, and in some form Latin satire with avidity. *Hamlet*, the *Malcontent*, and all the heroes of that type of play, "railed" continually. But with Webster every character and nearly every speech has something of the satirical outlook. They describe each other satirically. They are for ever girding at the conventional objects of satire, certain social follies and crimes. There are several little irrelevant scenes of satire, like the malevolent discussion of Count Malatesti (*D.M.*, III. 3). It is incessant. The topics are the ordinary ones, the painting of women, the ingratitude of princes, the swaggering of blusterers, the cowardice of pseudo-soldiers. It gives part of the peculiar atmosphere of these plays.

This rests on a side of Webster's nature, which, in combination with his extraordinary literary gifts, produces another queer characteristic of his—his fondness for, and skill in comment. He is rather more like a literary man trying to write for the theatre than any of his contemporaries. Theatrically, though he is competent and sometimes powerful, he exhibits no vastly unusual ability. It is his comments that bite deep. Such gems as Flamineo's description of Camillo:

"When he wears white satin one would take him by his black muzzle to be no other creature than a maggot;"

or of the Spanish ambassador:

"He carries his face in's ruff, as I have seen a serving man carry glasses in a cipress hat-band, monstrous steady, for fear of breaking: he looks like the claw of a black-bird, first salted, and then broiled in a candle;"

or Lodovico's of the black woman Zanche in love:

"Mark her, I prithee; she simpers like the suds
A collier hath been washed in;"

have frequently been quoted. They have a purely literary merit. In other places he achieves a dramatic effect, which would be a little less in a theatre than in the book, by comment. When Bosola brings the terrible discovery of the secret to Ferdinand and the Cardinal, he communicates it to them, unheard by us, up-stage. We only know, in reading, how they take it, by the comments of Pescara, Silvio, and

Delio, who are watching, down-stage—

PESC.   "Mark Prince Ferdinand:

A very salamander lives in's eye,

To mock the eager violence of fire."

SIL.   "That cardinal hath made more bad faces with
his oppression than ever Michael Angelo made good
ones: he lifts up's nose like a foul porpoise before a
storm."

PES.   "The Lord Ferdinand laughs."

DEL.   "Like a deadly cannon

That lightens ere it smokes . . ."

it goes straight to the nerves. "The Lord Ferdinand laughs."
It is unforgettable.

Webster had always, in his supreme moments, that trick
of playing directly on the nerves. It is the secret of Bosola's
tortures of the Duchess, and of much of Flamineo. Though
the popular conception of him is rather one of immense
gloom and perpetual preoccupation with death, his power
lies almost more in the intense, sometimes horrible, vigour
of some of his scenes, and his uncanny probing to the depths
of the heart. In his characters you see the instincts at work
jerking and actuating them, and emotions pouring out
irregularly, unconsciously, in floods or spurts and jets, driven
outward from within, as you sometimes do in real people.

The method of progression which Webster used in his

writing, from speech to speech or idea to idea, is curiously individual. The ideas do not develope into each other as in Shakespeare, nor are they tied together in neatly planned curves as in Beaumont and Fletcher. He seems to have, and we know he did, put them into the stream of thought from outside; plumping them down side by side. Yet the very cumbrousness of this adds, in a way, to the passion and force of his scenes, as a swift stream seems swifter and wilder when its course is broken by rocks and boulders. The craft of Shakespeare's genius moves with a speedy beauty like a yacht running close into the wind; Webster is a barge quanted slowly but incessantly along some canal, cumbrous but rather impressive.

This quality of the progression of Webster's thought, and, in part, of his language, contrasts curiously with his metre. The Elizabethan use of blank verse was always liable to be rather fine; but there was only a short period, and it was only in a few writers, that it got really free—until its final dissolution in the thirties. Webster was one of these writers, probably the freest. Only Shakespeare can approach him in the liberties he took with blank verse; but Shakespeare's liberties conformed to higher laws. Webster probably had a worse ear for metre, at least in blank verse, than any of his contemporaries. His verse is perpetually of a vague, troubled kind. Each line tends to have about ten syllables and about five feet. It looks in the distance like a blank verse line. Sometimes this line is extraordinarily successful; though it is never quite scannable. Brachiano's

"It is a word infinitely terrible,"

is tremendously moving. But sometimes Webster's metrical extravagance does not justify itself, and rather harasses. The trick of beginning a line with two unaccented syllables, if repeated too often in the same passage, does more to break the back of the metre than almost any other possible peculiarity.

On the whole it is probable that Webster did all this on purpose, seeing that a larger licence of metre suits blank verse in drama than is permissible in literature. When he turned poet, in *A Monumental Column*, he is equally unmetrical; but that can probably be attributed to the very strong influence of Donne. Certainly the lyrics in his plays would seem to show that as a lyric poet he could have been among the greatest, a master of every subtlety, at least of that lyric metre which he did use. It is the one which the Elizabethans, almost, invented, and upon which they performed an inconceivable variety of music. Milton, who learnt so much from them in this respect, made this metre the chief part of his heritage. But even he could not include all that various music. It is the metre of *L'Allegro*, *Il Penseroso*, and the end of *Comus*. No man ever got a stranger and more perfect melody from it than Webster in his dirges.

Webster's handling of a play, and his style of writing, have something rather slow and old-fashioned about them. He was not like Shakespeare or Beaumont and Fletcher, up-to-date and "slick." He worried his plays out with a grunting pertinacity. There are several uncouth characteristics of his that have an effect which halts between archaism and a kind of childish awkwardness, like "primitive" art of various nations and periods. Sometimes he achieves the same result it can have, of a simplicity and directness refreshingly different from later artifice and accomplishment. Sometimes he only seems, to the most kindly critic, to fail hopelessly for lack of skill.

One of these characteristics is the use of couplets, usually to end the scene, and commonly of a generalising nature. This is, of course, old-fashioned. The frequency of such couplets is an often-noticed feature of the early Elizabethan drama: and the plays of such a writer as Shakespeare are dated by the help of the percentage of rhyming to unrhyming lines. Even as late as Webster, other authors sometimes ended the play, or a scene, with a couplet. But they did it with grace; using it almost as a musical device, to bring the continued melody of their verse to a close. And in the earlier plays, where one or more rhyming couplets end most scenes and many speeches, and even, especially in the more lyrical parts, come into the middle of passages, the rest of the versification is of a simple, rhythmical end-stopped kind; and so the couplets seem scarcely different from the rest, a deeper shade of the same colour. Webster's couplets are electric green on crimson, a violent contrast with the rough, jerky, sketchy blank verse he generally uses. Some of them are so incongruous as to be ridiculous. At the end of a stormy passage with the Cardinal, Ferdinand says:

"In, in; I'll go sleep,
Till I know who leaps my sister, I'll not stir;
That known, I'll find scorpions to string my whips,
And fix her in a general eclipse." [*Exeunt.*

If you consider the general level of Webster's writing, this rings almost childish. In *The White Devil* there are two instances of rhyming couplets close to each other, one superbly successful, the other a failure. The rather hideous and queerly vital wooing-scene between Brachiano and Vittoria leads up to a speech of the former's that ends:

"You shall to me at once
Be dukedom, health, wife, children, friends, and all."

Cornelia, Vittoria's mother, who has been listening behind, unseen, breaks the tension with a rush forward and the cry:

"Woe to light hearts, they still forerun our fall!"

It has a Greek ring about it. It brings the fresh and terrible air of a larger moral world into the tiny passionate heat of that interview. And withal there is a run of fine music in the line. The rhyme helps all this materially. It enhances and marks the moment, and assists the play. But a dozen lines later, after some burning speeches of reproach in ordinary blank verse, Cornelia drops into rhyme again to show the moral of it all:

"See, the curse of children!
In life they keep us frequently in tears;
And in the cold grave leave us in pale fears."[1]

The end of the play affords even more extraordinary examples of these couplets. Sandwiched in between the dying Vittoria's tremendous

"My soul, like a ship in a black storm,
Is driven, I know not whither,"

and Flamineo's equally fine sentence—an example of generalisation rightly and nobly used—

"We cease to grieve, cease to be fortune's slaves,
Nay, cease to die, by dying,"

comes the smug and dapper irrelevancy of

"Prosperity doth bewitch men, seeming clear;
But seas do laugh, show white, when rocks are near."

It is beyond expression, the feeling of being let down, such couplets give one.

In three places a different and very queer side of Webster's old-fashionedness or of his occasional dramatic insensibility, is unpleasantly manifest. Here it becomes plainer, perhaps, that it is rather a childish than an old-fashioned tendency which betrays him to these faults. Three times, once in *The White Devil,* and twice in *The Duchess of Malfi,* the current of quick, living, realistic speeches—each character jerking out a hard, biting, dramatic sentence or two—is broken by long-winded, irrelevant, and fantastically unrealistic tales. They are of a sententious, simple kind, such as might appear in Æsop. Generally they seem to be lugged in by their ears into the play. They are introduced with the same bland, startling inconsequence with which some favourite song is brought into a musical comedy, but with immeasurably less justification. The instance in *The White Devil* is less bad than the others. Francisco is trying to stir Camillo against the indignity of horns. He suddenly tells him a long tale how Phœbus was going to be married, and the trades that don't like excessive heat made a deputation to Jupiter against the marriage, saying one sun was bad enough, they didn't want a lot of little ones. So, one Vittoria is bad enough; it is a good thing there are no children. It is pointless and foolish enough, in such a play. But the instances in *The Duchess of Malfi* surpass it. In the tremendous scene in the bedchamber when Ferdinand accuses the Duchess of her marriage, the mad frenzy of his reproaches is excellently rendered. She replies with short sentences, bursting from her heart. Each of his taunts carries flame. The whole is living, terse, and affecting. In the middle of this Ferdinand breaks into a long old-fashioned allegory about Love, Reputation, and Death, a tale that (but for a fine line or two) might have appeared in any Elizabethan collection of rhymed parables. The point of it is that Reputation is very easy to lose, and the Duchess has lost hers. It is as irrelevant and not so amusing as it would be if Michael Angelo had written a Christmas cracker posy on the scroll the Cumaean Sibyl holds. In the third instance the Duchess mars the end of a lovely and terrible scene (III. 5) by a would-be funny moral tale about a dogfish and a salmon. Here there is a sort of pathetic suitability in the Duchess, half broken with sorrow, almost unconsciously babbling childish tales to her enemies. But, with the other tales in mind, one finds it hard to believe Webster meant this. If he did, he did not bring his effect off. The tale is too incongruous with the rest of the scene.

There are still further instances of Webster's occasional extraordinary childishness in drama, namely his shameless use of asides, soliloquies, and other devices for telling his audience the motives of the actors or the state of the plot. The Elizabethans were always rather careless. The indiscriminate soliloquy or aside were part of their inheritance, which they but gradually got rid of. If soliloquies, and even asides, are handled rightly, in a kind of drama like the Elizabethan, they need not be blemishes. They can add greatly to the play.

Hamlet's soliloquies do. The trend of recent dramatic art has been unwise in totally condemning this stage device. There are two quite distinct effects of soliloquy in a play. One is to tell the audience the plot; the other is to let them see character or feel atmosphere. The first is bad, the second good. It is perfectly easy for an audience to accept the convention of a man uttering his thoughts aloud. It is even based on a real occurrence. When the man is alone on the stage it is an entirely simple and good convention. Even if there are other characters present, *i.e.* when the soliloquy approaches the aside, the trick only needs careful artistic handling. But the essential condition is that the audience feels it is *overhearing* the speaker, as much, at least, as it overhears the dialogue of the play. In soliloquies or in dialogues the characters may, to a certain extent, turn outward to the audience, and address them; in the same way as they forbear from often turning their backs on them. But soliloquies must go no further. So far, they are acceptable. If we can accept the extraordinary convention that a man's conversation shall be coherent, and in blank verse to boot, we can easily swallow his thoughts being communicated to us in the same way. It is only when the dramatist misuses this licence, and foists improbable and unnaturally conscious thoughts on a man, in order to explain his plot, that we feel restive. The fault, of course, lies in the unnaturalness and the shameless sudden appearance of the dramatist's own person, rather than in the form of a soliloquy. Only, soliloquies are especially liable to this. A legitimate and superb use of soliloquy occurs near the end of *The Duchess of Malfi*, in a passage from which I have already quoted, where the Cardinal enters, alone, reading a book:

"I am puzzled in a question about hell:
He says, in hell there's one material fire,
And yet it shall not burn all men alike,
Lay him by.
—How tedious is a guilty conscience!
When I look into the fish-pond in my garden,
Methinks I see a thing arm'd with a rake,
That seems to strike at me."
[*Enter* Bosola *and* Servant *bearing* Antonio's *body*.]

This is an entirely permissible and successful use of soliloquy. The words and thought are mysteriously thrilling. They sharpen the agony of the spectator's mind to a tense expectation; which is broken by the contrast of the swift purpose of Bosola's entry, with the servant and the body, and the violent progression of events ensuing. The whole is in tone together; and the effect bites deep, the feeling of the beginning of sheeting rain, breaking the gloomy pause before a thunderstorm. But there are cases of Webster using the soliloquy badly. In *The White Devil*, when the servant has told Francisco that Brachiano and Vittoria have fled the city together, he goes out. Francisco is left alone, exclaiming, "Fled! O, damnable!" He immediately alters his key:

"How fortunate are my wishes! Why, 'twas this
I only laboured! I did send the letter
To instruct him what to do," etc. etc.

One finds the dramatist rather too prominently and audibly there. But his presence becomes even more offensive when he is visible behind two characters and their dialogue, as in the instance from *The Devil's Law Case*, II. 1. A worse case of this, both in itself and because it comes in a tragedy, occurs in *The White Devil*, where Francisco and Monticelso explain their actions to each other, after Camillo, charged with the commission against the pirates, has made his exit.

FRANCISCO. "So, 'twas well fitted: now shall we discern
How his wish'd absence will give violent way
To Duke Brachiano's lust."

MONTICELSO.   "Why, that was it;
To what scorned purpose else should we make choice
Of him for a sea-captain?" etc.

But having informed us of their motives in this, Webster suddenly remembers that we may say, "But why should they start on such a line of action at all?" So Monticelso, later in the conversation, apropos of nothing in particular, remarks—

"It may be objected, I am dishonourable

To play thus with my kinsman; but I answer,
For my revenge I'd stake a brother's life,
That, being wrong'd, durst not avenge himself."

A very similar instance of a pathetic attempt to make the audience swallow the plot, by carefully explaining the motives, is in the fourth act of *The Duchess of Malfi*, a play distinctly less disfigured by these childishnesses of Webster's than *The White Devil*. There Ferdinand, in what purports to be a conversation with Bosola, goes back in his mind and rakes out, all unasked, his two motives for persecuting the Duchess. His behaviour, though badly portrayed, is less unconvincing and improbable than the *White Devil* instance. But such blunders make even the asides of Flamineo, when he is explaining his antic behaviour to the audience, flagrant as they are, seem mild and legitimate stage-devices.

A special class of unrealistic asides and conversations, and one very much affected by the Elizabethans, is the situation when A., B., and C. are on the stage, and B. and C. are carrying on a conversation, interspersed with asides between A. and B. which C. does not notice. People who have experience of the stage know how almost impossible this is to manage with any show of probability. In a comedy or farce the absurdity matters less. But the scene between Lodovico, Francisco, and Zanche, after Brachiano's death, though it partakes of farce, makes one uneasy.

All these childishnesses and blunders in Webster's plays, soliloquies, asides, generalisations, couplets, and the rest, are due, no doubt, to carelessness and technical incapacity. His gifts were of a different kind. But the continual generalisations arise also from a particular bent of his mind, and a special need he felt. It is normal in the human mind, it was unusually strong in the Elizabethans, and it found its summit in Webster of all of that time—the desire to discover the general rule your particular instance illustrates, and the delight of enunciating it. Many people find their only intellectual pleasure in life, in the continued practice of this. But drama seems, or seemed, to demand it with especial hunger; most of all the poetic drama. The Greeks felt this, and in the form of drama they developed this was one of the chief intellectual functions of the chorus. I say "intellectual," meaning that in their music and movement they appealed through other channels to the audience—though here, too, in part, to something the same taste in the audience, that is to say, the desire to feel a little disjunct from the individual case, and to view it against some sort of background. Metre itself has, psychologically, the same effect, a little. But the brain demands to be told τὸ μὴ φῦναι νικᾷ or μίμνει δὲ μίμνοντος ἐν χρόνῳ Διὸς παθεῖν τὸν ἔρξαντα, or any of the other deductions and rules.

The Greeks, then, received, to their satisfaction, the

knowledge of other instances or of the general rule or moral, from the chorus. It is interesting to see the various ways of achieving the effects of a chorus that later drama has used. For to some extent the need is always felt, though not violently enough to overcome the dramatic disadvantages of an actual chorus. Sometimes one character in a play is put aside to serve the purpose, like the holy man in Maxim Gorki's *The Lower Depths*. Or the characters sit down and, a little unrealistically, argue out their moral, as in Mr Shaw's plays. Mr Shaw and a good many modern German, English, and Scandinavian writers, also depend on the spectator having picked up, from prefaces and elsewhere, the general body of the author's views against the background of which any particular play is to be performed. Ibsen had two devices. One was to sum up the matter in some prominent and startling remark near the end, like the famous "People don't *do* such things!" The other was to have a half-mystical background, continually hinted at; the mountain-mines in *John Gabriel Borkman*, the heights in *When we Dead Awaken*, the sea in *The Lady from the Sea*, the wild duck. In certain catchwords these methods met; "homes for men and women," "ghosts," "you don't mean it!" and the rest. The temptation to point a moral in the last words of a play is almost irresistible; and sometimes justified. A well-known modern play called *Waste* ends, "The waste! the waste of it all!" The Elizabethans were very fond of doing this. They had the advantage that they could end with a rhymed couplet. But they were liable to do it at the end of any scene or episode. It has been pointed out how much Webster was addicted to this practice. Towards their close his plays became a string of passionate generalities. Antonio and Vittoria both die uttering warnings against "the courts of princes." Other characters alternate human cries at their own distress with great generalisations about life and death. These give to the hearts of the spectators such comfort and such an outlet for their confused pity and grief as music and a chorus afford in other cases. But Webster also felt the need of such broad moralising in the middle of his tragedies. Sometimes he pours through the mouth of such characters as Bosola and Flamineo, generalisation after dull generalisation, without illuminating. Greek choruses have failed in the same way. But when a gnome that *is* successful comes, it is worth the pains. The solidity and immensity of Webster's mind behind the incidents is revealed. Flamineo fills this part at the death of Brachiano. But often he and Bosola are a different, and very Websterian, chorus. Their ceaseless comments of indecency and mockery are used in some scenes to throw up by contrast and enhance by interpretation the passions and sufferings of human beings. They provide a background for Prometheus; but a background of entrails and vultures, not the cliffs of the Caucasus. The horror of suffering is intensified by such means till it is unbearable. The crisis of her travail comes on the tormented body and mind of the Duchess (II. 1) to the swift accompaniment of Bosola's mockery. Brachiano's wooing, and his later recapture, of Vittoria, take on the sick dreadfulness of figures in a nightmare, whose shadows parody them with obscene caricature; because of the ceaseless ape-like comments of Flamineo, cold, itchy, filthily knowing.

Light has interestingly been thrown of late on Webster's method of composition. It had long been known that he repeats a good many lines and phrases from himself and from other people: and that a great deal of his writing, especially in his best and most careful work, has the air of being proverbial, or excerpt. John Addington Symonds remarked with insight a good many years ago that Webster must have used a note-book. His plays read like it. And now Mr Crawford has discovered some of the sources he compiled his note-book from.[1] It would be useless to repeat Mr Crawford's list with a few additions, or to examine the instances one by one. Nearly, not quite, all his cases seem to me to be real ones. There are certainly quite enough to enable one to draw important inferences about Webster's way of working. These instances of borrowing are very numerous, and chiefly from two books, Sidney's *Arcadia*, and <u>Montaigne</u>—favourite sources of Elizabethan wisdom. They are very clearly marked, and consist in taking striking thoughts and phrases in the original, occasionally quite long ones, and rewriting them almost verbally, sometimes with slight changes to make them roughly metrical. It is a quite different matter from the faint "parallels" of ordinary commentators. I give one of the more striking instances, to illustrate:

***Arcadia*, Bk. II.:**

"But she, as if he had spoken of a small matter when he mentioned her life, to which she had not leisure to attend, desired him, if he loved her, to shew it in finding some way to save Antiphilus. For her, she found the world but a wearisome stage unto her, where she played a part against her will, and therefore besought him not to cast his love in so unfruitful a place as could not love itself. . . ."

***Arcadia*, Bk. III.:**

"It happened, at that time upon his bed, towards the dawning of the day, he heard one stir in his chamber, by the motion of garments, and with an angry voice asked who was there. 'A poor gentlewoman,' answered the party, 'that wish long life unto you,' 'And I soon death unto you,' said he, 'for the horrible curse you have given me.' "

***The Duchess of Malfi*, IV. 1 (p. 85):**

> DUCHESS.   "Who must dispatch me?
> I account this world a tedious theatre
> For I do play a part in't 'gainst my will."

125

BOSOLA. "Come, be of comfort; I will save your life."

DUCHESS. "Indeed, I have not leisure to tend
So small a business."

BOSOLA. "Now, by my life, I pity you."

DUCHESS. "Thou art a fool, then,
To waste thy pity on a thing so wretched
As cannot pity itself. I am full of daggers.
Puff, let me blow these vipers from me!
What are you?"

Enter Servant.

SERVANT. "One that wishes you long life."

DUCHESS. "I would thou wert hang'd for the horrible curse
Thou hast given me."

There are three explanations of all this. Either Webster knew
the *Arcadia* so well that he had a lot of it by heart. Or he had
the book and worked from it. Or he kept a note-book, into
which he had entered passages that struck him, and which
he used to write the play from. It seems to me certain that
the third is the true explanation. We know that Elizabethan
authors did sometimes keep note-books in this way. Bacon
did so, and Ben Jonson, whom Webster admired and rather
resembled, worked most methodically this way. The memory
theory could scarcely explain the verbal accuracy of so many
passages. But there are other considerations, which make the
note-book probable. The passages from the *Arcadia* or from

Montaigne came very often in lumps. You will get none, or only one or two, for some scenes, and then twenty lines or so that are a *cento* of them, carefully dovetailed and worked together. It is very difficult to imagine a man doing this from memory or from a book. But it is exactly what would happen if he were using a note-book which had several consecutive pages with *Arcadia* extracts, several more with Montaigne, and so on. The passage I quoted, which brings together an extract from *Arcadia*, III., and another from *Arcadia*, II., exemplifies this. But there are better instances. The first ten lines of *The Duchess of Malfi*, IV. 1 (p. 84), contain three continuous more or less verbal thefts from different parts of the *Arcadia*, the first and third from Book II., the second from Book I. Better still; in II. 1 (p. 67), Bosola has to utter some profound "contemplation," worthy of his malcontent type. Webster could not think of anything at the moment. He generally seems to have had recourse to his note-book when he was gravelled; for a lot of his borrowed passages make very little sense as they come in, and that of a rather sudden nature, in the way that generally betokens an interrupted train of thought. He went to his note-books on this occasion. He found, probably contiguous there, several sentences of a weighty, disconnected sense. They are from Montaigne, Florio's translation, pages 246, 249, 248, in that order.[1] Put together they have, as a matter of fact, very little meaning.

BOSOLA. "O, Sir, the opinion of wisdom is a foul tetter that runs all over a man's body; if simplicity direct us to have no evil it directs us to a happy being; for the subtlest folly proceeds from the subtlest wisdom; let me be simply honest."

Still, it did. And being at his Montaigne note-books, Webster went on. Bosola's next speech but one borrows from the first Book. For the long speech that follows it, he goes back to Book II.; and makes it entirely from two different passages, one on p. 239, one on p. 299.

A last instance is still more convincing. It concerns *A Monumental Column*, lines 23–35, and *The Duchess of Malfi*, III. 2 (p. 79), the description of Antonio. The first passage is mostly taken verbally from the two sources, Ben Jonson's Dedication to *A Masque of Queens* and the description of Musidorus in *Arcadia*, Book I. The passage in the play contains one of the same lines from Jonson, together with a different part of the sentence describing Musidorus, and a couple of lines from another part of *Arcadia*, Book I. And the remainder of the description of Musidorus duly turns up in *The Duchess of Malfi* a few scenes later, in IV. 1 (p. 84), sandwiched between two passages from *Arcadia*, Book II.

A good many of these passages Webster copied out identically, except sometimes for a few changes to make them go into rough verse. Others he altered in very interesting ways. It was not necessarily part of his goodness as an author to alter them. His genius comes out equally in the phrases he used to produce far greater effect than they do in the original, by putting them at some exactly suitable climax. We are getting beyond the attitude, born of the industrial age and the childish enthusiasm for property as such, which condemns such plagiarism, imitation, and borrowing. The Elizabethans had for the most part healthy and sensible views on the subject. They practised and encouraged the habit. When Langbaine, in his preface to *Momus Triumphans*, "condemns Plagiaries" (though he is only thinking of plots, even then), it is a sign of the decadence towards stupidity. The poet and the dramatist work with words, ideas, and phrases. It is ridiculous, and shows a wild incomprehension of the principles of literature, to demand that each should only use his own; every man's brain is filled by thoughts and words of other people's. Webster wanted to make Bosola say fine things. He had many in his mind or his note-book: some were borrowed, some his own. He put them down, and they answer their purpose splendidly.

"I stand like one
That long hath ta'en a sweet and golden dream;
I am angry with myself, now that I wake."

That was, or may have been, of his own invention.

"The weakest arm is strong enough that strikes
With the sword of justice."

That he had found in Sidney. There is no difference. In any case the first, original, passage was probably in part due to his friends' influence; and the words he used were originally wholly "plagiarised" from his mother or his nursemaid. "Originality" is only plagiarising from a great many.

So Webster reset other people's jewels and redoubled their lustre. "The soul must be held fast with one's teeth . . ." he found Montaigne remarkably saying in a stoical passage. The phrase stuck. Bosola, on the point of death, cries:[1]

"Yes I hold my weary soul in my teeth;
'Tis ready to part from me."

It is unforgettable.

Webster improved even Donne, in this way; in a passage of amazing, quiet, hopeless pathos, the parting of Antonio and the Duchess (*Duchess of Malfi*, III. 5), which is one long series of triumphant borrowings.:

"We seem ambitious God's whole work to undo;
Of nothing He made us, and we strive too
To bring ourselves to nothing back,"

Donne writes in *An Anatomy of the World*.

"Heaven fashion'd us of nothing; and we strive
To bring ourselves to nothing."

are Antonio's moving words.

This last example illustrates one kind of the changes other than metrical Webster used to make. He generally altered a word or two, with an extraordinarily sure touch, which proves his genius for literature. He gave the passages life and vigour, always harmonious with his own style. You see, by this chance side-light, the poet at work, with great vividness. "Fashion'd" for "made" here, is not a great improvement; but it brings the sentence curiously into the key of the rest of the scene. The metrical skill is astounding—the calm weight of "fashion'd"; the slight tremble of "Heaven" at the beginning of the line; the adaptation from Donne's stiff heavy combative accent, the line ending with "and we strive too," to the simpler easier cadence more suited to speech and to pathos, ". . . ; and we strive"; and the repetition of "nothing" in the same place in the two lines.

The long first example I gave of borrowing from Sidney gives good instances of change, among others the half-slangy vividness of

"Thou art a fool, then,
To waste thy pity on a thing so wretched
As cannot pity itself . . ."

for Sidney's mannered, dim,

"and therefore besought him not to cast his love in so unfruitful a place as could not love itself."

But the same places in *The Duchess of Malfi* and the *Arcadia* have a much finer example. The description of Queen Erona is transferred to the Duchess again. Sidney says that in her sorrow, one could "perceive the shape of loveliness more perfectly in woe than in joyfulness." Webster turned this, with a touch, to poetry in its sheerest beauty.

BOSOLA. "You may discern the shape of loveliness
More perfect in her tears than in her smiles."

It is just this substitution of the concrete for the abstract—which is the nearest one could get to a definition of the difference between a thought in good prose and the same thought in good poetry—that Webster excels in. Even where his adjectives gain, it is in this direction.

"Or is it true that thou wert never but a vain name, and no essential thing?"

says Sidney in a long passage on Virtue. Webster makes it a shade more visual, and twenty times as impressive:

"Or is it true thou art but a bare name,
And no essential thing?"

So Bosola gives life to a meditation of Montaigne. Montaigne's democratic mind pondered in his study on the essential equality of men. "We are deceived," he says of princes; "they are moved, stirred, and removed in their motions by the same springs and wards that we are in ours. The same reason that makes us chide and brawl and fall out with any of our neighbours, causeth a war to follow between princes; the same reason that makes us whip or beat a lackey maketh a prince (if he apprehend it) to spoil and waste a whole province. . . ." Bosola is the heart of democracy. "They are deceived, there's the same hand to them; the like passions sway them; the same reason that makes a vicar to go to law for a tithe-pig, and undo his neighbours, makes them spoil a whole province, and batter down goodly cities with the cannon." The tithe-pig carries you on to Parnassus; Bosola has the vision of an artist.

The liveliness of the "there's" for "there is" in the last quotation is typical. Webster, like all the great Elizabethans, knew he was writing for the ear and not the eye. They kept in close touch, in their phrases, rhythms, and turns, with speech. Their language was greater than speech, but it was in that kind; it was not literature.

But there is one example of adoption and adaptation where Webster stands out quite clear as the poet, with the queer and little-known mental processes of that kind of man suddenly brought to the light. Montaigne has a passage:

"Forasmuch as our sight, being altered, represents unto itself things alike; and we imagine that things fail it as it doth to them: As they who travel by sea, to whom mountains, fields, towns, heaven, and earth, seem to go the same motion, and keep the same course they do."

The sense is clear and on the surface. He is illustrating

the general rule by an interesting instance from ordinary experience. When you go in a train, or a boat, the sky, the earth, and its various features, all seem to be moving in one direction.[1] In *The White Devil* Flamineo is tempting Vittoria with the happiness Brachiano can give her.

"So perfect shall be thy happiness, that, as men at sea think land and trees and ships go that way they go, so both heaven and earth shall seem to go your voyage."

Webster took this instance of Montaigne's and used it to help out quite a different sense. He used it as a simile of that elusive, unobvious, imaginative kind that illuminates the more that you can scarcely grasp the point of comparison. But he did more. He was led to it by thinking, as a poet thinks, only half in ideas and half in words. Or rather, with ordinary people, ideas lead to one another, suggest one another, through ideas. With poets they do it through words, quite illogically. The paths of association in the brain are different in the two cases. A word is an idea with an atmosphere, a hard core with a fringe round it, like an oyster with a beard, or Professor William James' conception of a state of mind. Poets think of the fringes, other people of the core only. More definitely, if the dictionary meaning of a word is a and the atmosphere x, the poet thinks of it as $(x + a)$, and his trains of thought are apt to go on accordingly. So here, Webster found, vaguely, "heaven and earth" . . . "going the same motion" . . . and he leapt to the mystical conception of supreme happiness. He took "heaven and earth" from their original, half material, significance, and transfigured them. He took them from the illustration and put them into the thing illustrated. The meaning of the original suggested one thing to his mind, the words another; he combined them, in another world. And the result is a simile of incomprehensible appropriateness and exquisite beauty, an idea in a Shelleyan altitude where words have various radiance rather than meaning, an amazing description of the sheer summit of the ecstacy of joy.

The note-book habit suited those idiosyncrasies of Webster's slow-moving mind which distinguished him from the ready rhetoric of Fletcher and the perpetual inspiration of Shakespeare. The use of such a thing by a poet implies a difference from other poets in psychology, not, as is often ignorantly supposed, in degree of merit. It merely means he has a worse memory. All writers are continually noting or inventing phrases and ideas, which form the stuff from which their later inspiration chooses. Some have to note them down, else they slip away for ever. Others can note them in their mind and yet feel secure of retaining them. The advantage of this method is that you unconsciously transmute all "borrowed" ideas to harmony with your own personality—that when you hunt them out to reclaim them you find them slightly changed. The disadvantage, under modern conditions, is that you may commit the most terrible sin of plagiarism, and lift another man's work, and display it in a recognisable form, without knowing it. So Meredith in one of his last and best lyrics, an eight-lined poem called "Youth and Age," repects a line identically from Swinburne's best poem, *The Triumph of Time*; and all unconsciously. The disadvantage of the note-book method is that you have to perform the operation of digesting your trophy, harmonising it with the rest of the work, on the spot. Webster does not always do this successfully. There are passages, as we have seen, where he too flagrantly helps himself along with his note-book. But as a rule he weaves in his quotations extraordinarily well; they become part of the texture of the play, adding richness of hue and strength of fabric. In *The White Devil*, in the scene of astounding tragical farce where Flamineo persuades Vittoria and Zanche to try to murder him with bulletless pistols, the quotations from Montaigne come in entirely pat. For it is not, generally, when the play goes slowest that Webster has most recourse to his note-book. The swift passion of Ferdinand's interview with the guilty Duchess (*Duchess of Malfi*, III. 2) is, if you enquire closely, entirely composed of slightly altered passages from the *Arcadia*. This detracts no whit from its tumultuous force.

The chief value of working through a note-book, from a literary point of view, is this. A man tends to collect quotations, phrases, and ideas, that particularly appeal to and fit in with his own personality. If that personality is a strong one, and the point of his work is the pungency with which it is imbued with this strong taste, the not too injudicious agglutination of these external fragments will vastly enrich and heighten the total effect. And this is, on the whole, what happens with Webster. The heaping-up of images and phrases helps to confuse and impress the hearer, and gives body to a taste that might otherwise have been too thin to carry. Webster, in fine, belongs to the caddis-worm school of writers, who do not become their complete selves until they are incrusted with a thousand orts and chips and fragments from the world around.

It would be possible to go on for a long time classifying various characteristics of Webster, and discovering them in different passages or incidents in his plays. And it would be possible, too, to lay one's finger on several natural reactions and permanent associations in that brain. All have noticed his continual brooding over death. He was, more particularly, obsessed by the idea of the violence of the moment of death. Soul and body appeared to him so interlaced that he could not conceive of their separation without a struggle and pain. Again, his mind was always turning to metaphors of storms and bad weather, and especially the phenomenon of lightning. He is for ever speaking of men lightening to speech or action; he saw words as the flash from the thundercloud of wrath or passion.

But, after all, the chief characteristic of Webster's two plays and of many things in those plays, is that they are good; and the chief characteristic of Webster is that he is a good dramatist. The great thing about *The Duchess of Malfi* is that it is the material for a superb play; the great thing about the fine or noble things in it is not that they illustrate anything or belong to any class, but, in each case, the fine and noble thing itself. All one could do would be to print them out at length; and this is no place for that; it is easier to buy Webster's works (though, in this scandalous country, not very easy). The end of the matter is that Webster was a great writer; and the way in which one uses great writers is two-fold. There is the exhilarating way of reading their writing; and there is the essence of the whole man, or of the man's whole work, which you carry away and permanently keep with you. This essence generally presents itself more or less in the form of a view of the universe, recognisable rather by its emotional than by its logical content. The world called Webster is a peculiar one. It is inhabited by people driven, like animals, and perhaps like men, only by their instincts, but more blindly and ruinously. Life there seems to flow into its forms and shapes with an irregular abnormal and horrible volume. That is ultimately the most sickly, distressing feature of Webster's characters, their foul and indestructible vitality. It fills one with the repulsion one feels at the unending soulless energy that heaves and pulses through the lowest forms of life. They kill, love, torture one another blindly and without ceasing. A play of Webster's is full of the feverish and ghastly turmoil of a nest of maggots. Maggots are what the inhabitants of this universe most suggest and resemble. The sight of their fever is only alleviated by the permanent calm, unfriendly summits and darknesses of the background of death and doom. For that is equally a part of Webster's universe. Human beings are writhing grubs in an immense night. And the night is without stars or moon. But it has sometimes a certain quietude in its darkness; but not very much.

[1] This couplet seems even absurder to us than it should, because the word "frequently" has since Webster got a rapid colloquial sense of "quite often."

[1] Crawford, *Collectanea*, i. 20–46, ii 1–63.

[1] Professor Henry Morley's reprint.

[1] It is only because there are scores of other certain borrowings of Webster from Montaigne that I accept this one. By itself it would not be a convincing plagiarism.

[1] Note, though, that Montaigne has made a slip. They

really appear to be moving in the *opposite* direction to yourself. Webster takes the idea over, mistake and all.

APPENDICES.

THE AUTHORSHIP OF THE LATER
"APPIUS AND VIRGINIA."[1]

IT is startlingly obvious, and has been remarked by every critic of Webster, that *Appius and Virginia* is quite different from his other plays. It "stands apart from the other plays," says Professor Vaughan.[2] Dr Ward recognises it as a work of Webster's "later manhood, if not of his old age." Mr William Archer vastly prefers it to the ordinary crude Websterian melodrama. In fact, critics, whether of the Elizabethans in general or of Webster in particular, have always exhibited either conscious discomfort or unconscious haste and lack of interest, when they came to this play. As they have never questioned its authenticity, their perfunctory and unprofitable treatment of it is noteworthy. They cannot fit it in. In summing up Webster's characteristics, they have either quietly let it slide out of sight, or else brought it formally and unhelpfully in, to sit awkward and silent among the rest like a deaf unpleasant aunt at a party of the other side of the family. But never, so far as I am aware, has anyone suggested that it is not by Webster.

We may sympathise with the critics. The more closely *Appius and Virginia* is looked at, the less it shows of the Webster we know. With *Northward Ho* and *Westward Ho*, one is not discomforted at finding almost no such mark. You may imagine Webster a young man, collaborating with an older, in a well-defined, not very congenial, type of play, contributing the smaller part. There are a hundred reasons against what we mean by Webster being prominent in those plays. Anyhow, a young man's work is frequently anybody's; especially his hack-work. Who could pick out Meredith's war correspondence from anyone else's? But once he has developed his particular savour, it can hardly fade into commonness again. It is as with faces. You can often mistake two young faces. But once the soul has got to work, wrinkling and individualising the countenance, it remains itself for ever, even after the soul has gone. The taste we recognise as Webster developed between 1607 and 1615. It is a clinging, unmistakable one. Later on he imitated models who provoked it less powerfully. But a close, long scrutiny, before which *Appius and Virginia* grows more cold and strange, increasingly reveals Webster in *The Devil's Law-*

Case, even in *A Cure for a Cuckold*, of which he only wrote part.

Examine *Appius and Virginia* æsthetically and as a whole. Webster is a dogged, slow writer, and romantic—in the sense that single scenes, passages, or lines have merit and intensity on their own account. As a rule, he finely proves that quintessence of the faith that the God of Romanticism revealed to his inattentive prophet. "Load every rift with ore." And there is a kind of dusty heat over all. *Appius and Virginia* is precisely the opposite. Its impression is simple and cool. It seems more an effort at classicism—unconscious perhaps. There are not many lines or images you stop over. You see right to the end of the road.

It is, of course, a very poor argument against attributing a play to any particular author, that he has not written this kind of play elsewhere. The very fact that he hasn't, makes it all the harder to know what his attempt in this manner *would* be like. And when such an argument is used, as it is, to prove that *A Yorkshire Tragedy* is not Shakespeare's, it is of no value, though it may be on the right side. What is permissible, however, is, when a writer has several distinct characteristics, to expect to recognise some of them, when he is seriously attempting a kind of play not very different from his ordinary one; especially if these characteristics are of certain kinds. A mere journalist, turning out his daily task, may sometimes write an indistinguishable undistinguished play in a different style. A great master of a certain type may possibly, his tongue just perceptibly bulging the cheek, flash out something quite good in an entirely other kind, as a *tour de force*. Or a very brilliant and not at all serious person, with a trick of writing, some *Græculus* of literature, may sink his own personality entirely in the manner of another. But that is only possible if he is able to aim entirely at parody, and not at all at art. Few artists could ever do this. In any case, Webster and *Appius and Virginia* do not fit into any of these potential explanations. He worked (as he tells us, and we can see) slowly and with trouble. Both his method and the result show that he was no easily adaptable writer. His clumsy, individual, passionate form betrays itself under borrowed clothes. This does not mean that he strode always intensely and unswervingly along his own path. He was, in an odd way, ready enough to put on other people's clothes that did not suit him. But they never fitted all over. It is suggested that in *Appius and Virginia* he was trying to imitate Shakespeare's Roman tragedies. This might explain the absence of some of his peculiarities, and the presence of other marks; the change of atmosphere, the greater number of rhyming lines, and so forth. But subtler questions of metre and vocabulary go deeper, in proportion as they are more unconscious. consideration of such delicate points, together with a careful general æsthetic tasting of the whole play, seem to me to warrant a very strong critical doubt whether Webster wrote *Appius and Virginia*.

The characters of the play are slight and ordinary. The clown is quite unlike anything we could expect Webster to invent. Appius, the Machiavellian villain, has a little fire. Virginius is a mere stage-creature, and, as that, quite creditable. Virginia is a virgin. The crowd of soldiers is a soldiers' crowd. Webster's characters, in the other plays, if they do not always (compared at least with Shakespeare's) make a highly individual impression on the mind, always leave a dent.

The metre of *Appius and Virginia* is not Webster's. The blank verse is much stricter. Webster's loose, impressionistic iambics, with their vague equivalence and generous handling, are very unlike these regular, rhetorical lines. Webster's great characteristic of beginning a line with what classical prosodists would call an anapæst finds no place here. And the general metrical technique of which this is only the most obvious manifestation—the continual use of substitution and equivalence in the feet, or, better, the thinking more in lines and less in feet[1]—is strikingly absent in *Appius and Virginia*. These prosodic habits are also almost as little prominent in the possibly Websterian part of *A Cure for a Cuckold*. But there is another point which marks *Appius and*

145

Virginia off from all the rest. In the other plays, there is little attempt to keep a line that is divided between two speakers pentametrical. If one speech ends with a line of two and a half feet, the next may begin with a line of two feet, or of three, or with a complete line. *Appius and Virginia* keeps almost invariably to the old tradition, by which the speeches dovetail perfectly.[2]

The first and almost the only characteristic in this play to strike a casual reader, is the vocabulary. It is full of rare Latin words, mostly wearing an air of recent manufacture; "to deject" (in a literal sense), "munition," "invasive," "devolved," "donative," "palpèd," "enthronised," "torvèd," "strage," and many more. This particular vocabulary is a mark of certain writers, especially of the period at the end of the sixteenth and beginning of the seventeenth centuries, which had a joyous fertility in inventing new words that soon drooped and grew sterile. It was mostly employed by the slightly classicist authors. Of the major dramatists, Ben Jonson had a touch of it; Marston, Heywood, Chapman, and Shakespeare show it chiefly. Shakespeare has this variety among all his other varieties, neologisms, and ἅπαξ λεγόμενα: Chapman and Heywood this in especial.

In this and every notable respect the language of *Appius and Virginia* is unlike Webster's. Whatever linguistic point of detail you choose, the lack of resemblance is obvious. To take one instance: Dr Stoll (p. 40), in trying to prove the Webster authorship of the major part of *A Cure for a Cuckold*, uses as a test the occurrence of the exclamation "Ha!" especially as comprehending a whole speech. He says it is unusually frequent in Webster. "It appears in *The White Devil* thirteen times, six of them being whole speeches; in *Malfi* ten times, two of them whole speeches; in the *Law-Case* nine times, four of them whole speeches; in *Appius and Virginia* twice; in the main plot of the *Cure for a Cuckold* seven times, two of them whole speeches." The oddness of the *Appius and Virginia* figures does not strike Dr Stoll, who is on other business. He explains them, vaguely, by "the frigidity and academic character of the play"; which is far from fair to the slightly Marlovian and "Machiavellian" nature of much of *Appius and Virginia*. It is not a Jonsonian Roman play. There is no reason why Appius should not have said "Ha!" thirteen times, six of them whole speeches, except that the author did not write like that.

Again, the word "foul" was, characteristically, a common one with Webster. It occurs often in *The White Devil*, on almost every page in *The Duchess of Malfi*. "Think on your cause," says Contarino to Ercole in *The Devil's Law-Case*, II. 2; "It is a wondrous foul one." And when the real "devil's law-case" comes on (IV. 2), the shameless Winifred desires, "Question me in Latin, for the cause is very foul." There was this habit in Webster of thinking of such moral rottenness as "foul," slightly materialising it. A reader would feel safe in betting that Webster would use the word several times in connection with the trial of Virginia. One knows his comment on it, as one knows how a friend will take a piece of news. The word does not occur in this passage.

Analysis might find a thousand more points, positive and negative, in which the style and vocabulary of *Appius and Virginia* are obviously not those of Webster. The dissimilarity becomes still more obvious when the language is unanalytically tasted as a whole. It is throughout rhetorical and easy, with a slight permanent artificiality. The style is rather imitative of Shakespeare's, and alive, but not kicking.

In the general construction and handling of the play there is an un-Websterian childishness and crudity. Webster could be *gauche* enough at times, but not in this shallow, easy way. I need only enumerate some of the instances.

The Elizabethans were splendidly unsubservient to time. But the better dramatists tended to conceal their freedom; Webster among them. The keenestwitted spectator of *A Midsummer Night's Dream* or *The Merchant of Venice* could not, unless he were looking for them, discern the tricks Shakespeare has played with time. The instance in *Appius and Virginia* is far more flagrant, though it might strike an Elizabethan less than us. Act V. scene 3 takes place in the prison. Icilius, seeing Virginius relent towards Appius, vanishes to fetch the body of Virginia. *Seven lines after his exit*, a shout is heard. It turns out that in this time Icilius has gone through the streets to where Virginia is lying, taken up the body, and started back through the streets carrying it; and the people have begun to make an uproar. Eleven lines later, Icilius enters with the body. If the play stands as it was written, it is difficult to believe that Webster could have committed such absurdities. They might possibly, but not probably, be explained by a theory, for which there is other evidence, that we have the play in a cut and revised state.[1] But nothing can be thought too childish to come from the author of the crowd-effects in Act II. 2, where the First Soldier asks:

Soldiers, shall I relate the grievances

Of the whole regiment?

You might expect *Omnes* to answer "Yes!" or "No!" if they were all agreed. It is too startling when, with one voice, they cry "Boldly!" But a more amazing instance of sympathy and intelligence follows. The First Soldier ends a piece of rhetoric with:

from thence arise

A plague to choke all Rome!

OMNES. And all the suburbs!

There is a childishness that goes deeper, in the handling

149

of the plot and episodes. It is all told with a forthright and unthinking simplicity that is quite different from any Chapmanesque stark directness; the simplicity of a child who wants to tell a story, not of an artist who grasps the whole. It is apparent in the soliloquies of II. 1, in the end of I. 3, and especially at the beginning of the same scene, in the interview between Marcus and Appius. Appius is melancholy, declares himself in love. Marcus asks with whom, offering to act pander. Appius tells him, Virginia.

MARCUS. Virginia's!

APPIUS. Hers.

MARCUS.   I have already found

An easy path which you may safely tread,

Yet no man trace you.

He goes on to explain in detail his rather elaborate plan.

It is difficult to imagine dramatic innocence of this kind coming from Webster, whose humour and *bizarrerie* are, if not always successful, always entirely conscious, and whose simplicity, as playwright, is rather archaistic than childish.

These are some of the immediate difficulties in believing *Appius and Virginia* to be by Webster. The further difficulties of explaining the nature and date of the play, if it is by him, strengthen our incredulity. *How* Webster came to write such a play, his various critics and commentators have not tried to explain; chiefly because they have not understood that there was any need of explanation. They have realised neither how astonishing a *tour de force* it is, for an author so completely to sink his personality, nor that Webster is the last man to be capable of such a feat. The dumb evidence of their inability to make this play fit in with or illuminate the rest of Webster's work, speaks for them. *When* Webster wrote it, is a question they have tried to answer, however dimly. Their answers have all been different, and all importantly unconvincing. In the first place, the whole style of the play, in plot, characterisation, and metre, suggests an early date, somewhere between 1595 and 1615; and joins it, loosely, with *Julius Cæsar* (1601?), *Coriolanus* (1608?) and Heywood's *The Rape of Lucrece* (1604?). This is especially to be remarked of the metre, which is rather formal, without being stiff. It has few "equivalences," that is to say, the lines have nearly always ten (or, if "feminine," eleven) syllables. The licences are regular. They mostly consist of a few limited cases in which elision occurs, always noticeably, and almost conventionally—the chief example is between "to" and a verb beginning with a vowel.[1] I have already noticed the metrical dovetailing of speeches. All these prosodic characteristics suit, some rather demand, a date between 1600 and 1610. So does the influence of Marlowe and Machiavellism, and the character of the clown, Corbulo, who is staringly introduced into the original story. Finally, the general and specific dissimilarity in style of *Appius and Virginia* and Webster's other plays forbids a middle date, and requires an early rather than a late one, if the play be his. Only a young hand could have disguised its individuality so completely.

The other evidence, however, points in precisely the opposite direction. When you try to suggest a possible date you meet bewildering difficulties. One of the most certain things about *Appius and Virginia* is that it is strongly influenced by Shakespeare's Roman plays, and especially by *Coriolanus*.[2] *Coriolanus* is dated by most critical opinion as 1608-9. So *Appius and Virginia* must be at least as late as 1609. But that is definitely in Webster's middle, most individual, period. *The White Devil* appeared in 1611, and he was confessedly a long time in writing it. If the author of *The White Devil* wrote *Appius and Virginia*, it cannot have been only a year or eighteen months before. Then again you cannot slip the Roman play amazingly between *The White Devil* and *The Duchess of Malfi* (c. 1613). It would be far easier to say that Shakespeare wrote *Titus Andronicus* between *As You Like It* and *Twelfth Night*. And you must leave a decent interval after *The Duchess of Malfi*. You feel inclined to drop it quietly in the vacant space between *The Duchess of Malfi* and *The Devil's Law-Case*. But the progression in style here is so clear and gradual that it is nearly as difficult to squeeze it in there as between the tragedies. Besides, if you get as late as 1617 or 1618, you may as well listen to Dr Stoll's evidence—that it is not mentioned in Webster's dedication to *The Devil's Law-Case* (printed 1623), and that it shows such close debts to Shakespeare that Webster must have written it after reading the First Folio (1623). So, buffeted and confused, you take refuge in his spacious "1623-1639"; a date which is in direct opposition to all your first conclusions. And if you want to adorn the affair, now you have settled it, with the circumstance and charm of reality, you may attribute, with Dr Stoll, not only Webster's style and handling to his study of the First Folio, but his Marlowe characteristics to his recent study of *The Massacre at Paris* (1593) preparatory to writing his own play *The Guise*, his clown to his friendship with Heywood, his strange style to his imitativeness of the fashion of his time, and his writing this sort of play at all to his fancy for going back to the fashions of twenty or thirty years earlier!

II

Well then, what reasons are there for thinking that Webster did write *Appius and Virginia*? The reasons are two—the attribution in 1654, and repetitions or parallels between Webster's other plays and this. They require examination.

Appius and Virginia was printed and published in 1654,

as by John Webster. The same edition was put forth in 1659 with a new title-page "Printed for Humphrey Moseley";[1] and again in 1679, "Acted at the Duke's Theatre under the name of *The Roman Virgin* or *Unjust Judge.*" It is possible that Moseley only took over the edition between 1654 and 1659. In that case the attribution has even less weight. But let us put it at its strongest and suppose (what is most probable) that Moseley was always the publisher. It is being realised more and more how little importance attributions of the second half of the seventeenth century have. The theatrical traditions had been broken. Publishers attributed by guess-work, or hearsay, or to sell the book. In 1661, Kirkman published *The Thracian Wonder* as by Webster and Rowley. "No one," says Professor Vaughan, "except the editor, has ever supposed that Webster can have had a hand in it." Yet it is as Websterian as *Appius and Virginia*. The truth is, critics have at the back of their minds an idea that good poets write good poetry, and bad poets write bad poetry. Since this is as far as they can get, they are ready to give any good poem or play to any good poet, and to refuse any bad one. *Appius and Virginia* being a fairly good play, there is no reason in the world why it should not be the work of Webster, who was a good writer. *The Thracian Wonder*, a bad play, could not possibly be from that hand. . . . The truth is very different. In actuality, a good poet or playwright tends to write good and bad things in his own style. An examination of the works of poets we can be sure about—Keats, or Shelley, or Swinburne—shows this. The author of the sonnet *On first looking into Chapman's Homer* and the *Ode to a Nightingale* also wrote the sonnets *To my Brother George* and to *G.A.W.* If the work of a century ago were largely anonymous or doubtful, and if the principles of Elizabethan criticism were applied, he might be given *Alastor* or *The Vision of Judgement*; he would certainly be robbed of the sonnets to George Keats and Georgina Wylie.

Humphrey Moseley was, as a matter of fact, one of the more trustworthy publishers of the time. Malone and Professor Parrott are too hard on him. But he had the faults and ignorance of his period. Among other attributions he gives *The Merry Devil of Edmonton* to Shakespeare, *The Parliament of Love* (Massinger) to Rowley, *The Faithful Friends* to Beaumont and Fletcher, *Alphonsus, Emperor of Germany* to Chapman, *The Widow* (Middleton) to Jonson, Fletcher, and Middleton, *Henry I* and *Henry II* (Davenport, probably) to Shakespeare and Davenport, and *The History of King Stephen, Duke Humphrey,* and *Iphis and Iantha* to Shakespeare.

Webster's works have, in one way and another, been pretty thoroughly scrutinised for parallels. Resemblances in phrasing and thought between *The White Devil, The Duchess* of *Malfi*, *The Devil's Law-Case*, and *A Monumental Column* are very numerous. *A Cure for a Cuckold* and *Appius and Virginia* are far less closely joined. In *A Cure for a Cuckold* there are certain minor echoes of phrase that have some weight. I give a list of the only connections of *Appius and Virginia* with the other plays that have been discovered previously, or that I have found.[1]

(*a*) *Appius and Virginia*, 149:

I have seen children oft eat sweetmeats thus,

As fearful to devour them:

Duchess of Malfi, 65:

I have seen children oft eat sweetmeats thus,

As fearful to devour them too soon.

(*b*) *A. and V.*, 151:

One whose mind

Appears more like a ceremonious chapel

Full of sweet music, than a thronging presence.

Duchess of Malfi, 79:

His breast was filled with all perfection,

And yet it seemed a private whispering-room

It made so little noise of 't.

Monumental Column, II. 78, 79:

Who had his breast instated with the choice

Of virtues, though they made no ambitious noise.

(*c*) *A. and V.*, 163:

VIRGINIA. But she hath a matchless eye, Sir.

CORBULO. True, her eyes are no right matches.

White Devil, 31:

BRACHIANO. Are not those matchless eyes mine?

VITTORIA.   I had
rather
They were not matches.[1]

(*d*) *A. and V.*, 165:

I only give you my opinion,
I ask no fee for 't.

Westward Ho! 242:

Take my counsel: I'll ask no fee for 't.

White Devil, 7:

This is my counsel and I'll ask no fee for 't.

(*e*) *A. and V.*, 168:

As aconitum, a strong poison, brings
A present cure against all serpents' stings.

White Devil, 26:

Physicians, that cure poisons, still do work
With counter-poisons.

(*f*) *A. and V.*, 171:

I vow this is a practised dialogue:
Comes it not rarely off?

Duchess of Malfi, 63:

I think this speech between you both was studied,

It came so roundly off.

(*g*) *A. and V.*, 172:

For we wot

The office of a Justice is perverted quite

When one thief hangs another.[1]

Duchess of Malfi, 90:

The office of justice is perverted quite

When one thief hangs another.

(*h*) *A. and V.*, 180:

Death is terrible

Unto a conscience that's oppressed with guilt!

Duchess of Malfi, 99:

How tedious is a guilty conscience!

(*i*) *A. and V.*, 173:

I have sung

With an unskilful, yet a willing voice,

To bring my girl asleep.

White Devil, 45:

I'll tie a garland here about his head;

'Twill keep my boy from lightning.

Besides these, there are various words; "dunghill" (*A. and V.*, 171, 166, *White Devil*, 25), "mist" (of ignorance) (*A. and V.*, 167, 170, *White Devil*, 50[1]) are favourite and typical words of Webster. Note also "pursenet" in the sense of "wile" (*A. and V.*, 170, *Devil's Law-Case*, 130) and "not-being" (*A.*

and V., 180, *Duchess of Malfi*, 90).

Of the resemblances, (*c*) is a common joke, (*e*) a common idea (the Ben Jonson, *Sejanus*, quotation which Dyce gives in a note is much nearer than the passage from the *White Devil* to the *A. and V.* quotation), and (*d*) sounds like a catch-phrase. In (*h*) the two examples occur near the end of their plays, and slightly recall each other in atmosphere. In (*i*) the same effect of tenderness is got by the word "my."

It seems to me that (*b*), a suggestion of Mr Crawford's, holds good only between *The Duchess of Malfi* and *A Monumental Column*.

These six examples are such that they would be important if they were ten or fifteen times as numerous; being so few they are of no account. And I do not think many more could be found.

The rest, (*a*), (*f*) and (*g*), are another matter. It is to be noted that (*a*) and (*g*) are exactly the sort of images and proverbial sayings (note the expression "we wot") that Webster and others collected. If Webster wrote *Appius and Virginia*, we can only say that he must have used the same note-book that he wrote *The Duchess of Malfi* with. If not, either the author of *Appius and Virginia* compiled *his* note-book out of *The Duchess of Malfi* among other books; or else they used common sources. (*f*) is an even more significant parallel. For the circumstances are similar. In each drama two "villains" play into each other's hands in a dialogue which the "hero" discerns, suddenly, or guesses, to have been rehearsed. It is not an obvious thought. That it should be expressed at all is noteworthy; that it should be expressed with such similiarity of phrase and (which is important) metrical setting, is a valuable proof of identity of authorship.

The words have little weight. The use of "mist" is striking; but "dunghill," though it irresistibly recalls Webster's manner, was not monopolised by him; and "not-being" (the repetition of which Dr Stoll seems to think remarkable) is not rare enough or typical enough to be of any significance.

There the proofs of Webster's authorship end. The attribution of a late publisher, which is evidence of a notoriously untrustworthy character, and three or four passages of repetition or resemblance—that is all. The conclusion, for any impartial mind, is that there is very little evidence of the play being Webster's, rather more for his having had a finger in it, but much stronger evidence still that he had practically nothing to do with it.

III

If that is all there is to be said, we are left with an impression of general confusion, and a strongish feeling that anyhow Webster is responsible for very little of the play.

But the question would be cleared, if anyone discovered a more promising candidate. This I believe I have done. I think I can show that *Appius and Virginia* is largely, or entirely, the work of Thomas Heywood. I shall give the direct proofs first: then the more indirect ones, by showing how his authorship fits in with the various facts that have made such havoc of Webster's claims.

I have mentioned the queer distinctive vocabulary, especially of Latin words, used in *Appius and Virginia*. The fact that Heywood uses a very similar vocabulary, especially in all his more classical works, would of itself be of little weight. But an individual examination of all the very unusual words and phrases in this play, together with a hurried scrutiny of Heywood's dramas, provides very startling results. I give a list. More minute search, no doubt, might largely increase it. It serves its purpose. I begin with the more striking words.[1]

A. and V., 179:

Redeem a base life with a noble death,

And through your lust-burnt veins *confine* your breath.

"Confine," in this sense of "banish," was very rare. The *N.E.D.* gives one more or less contemporary example from Holinshed, and one, the only one, from Shakespeare. Dyce, in a footnote, gives five passages; he comments, "it is somewhat remarkable that they are all from Heywood." I can add two. It was a very special word of Heywood's.

Pleasant Dialogues, ii. p. 115:

The soul *confine*,

The body's dead, nor canst thou call it thine.

Royal King and Loyal Subject, 82:

Which as your gift I'll keep, till Heaven and Nature

Confine it hence.

It is to be noticed that the context in these two examples is similar.

Other examples are in *The Golden Age*, 23, *The Rape of Lucrece*, 242, *A Challenge for Beauty*, 10, *The Brazen Age*, 199, Γυναικεῖον, iv, 207.

A. and V., 174:

If the general's heart be so *obdure*.

"Obdure" is a very rare word. It does not occur in Shakespeare. In the Elizabethan age it seems to have been used only by one or two religious writers and Heywood. Heywood is always using it. This word alone might almost be accepted as a proof that the passage it occurs in was by him.

"Obdure" as adjective occurs in *Lucrece*, 219, 224, *Golden Age*, 56, 60, *Fortune by Land and Sea*, 375, *Pleasant Dialogues*, 114: as verb, *English Traveller*, 90, Γυναικαῖου, i. 55, *Brit. Troy*, vi. 11. "Obdureness" comes in Γυναικαῖου, i, 55.

A. and V., 162: "*Palpèd*."

There are only three known instances of this extraordinary word; this one, and two from Heywood's acknowledged works: *Brit. Troy*, xv. xlii. and *Brazen Age*, 206.

I add a short list of instances that are less persuasive individually, but have enormous weight collectively.

A. and V., 152:

Why should my lord droop, or *deject* his eye?

Rare in this literal sense: not in Shakespeare. Heywood. *If you know not me*, 206:

It becomes not

You, being a Princess, to *deject* your knee.

Cf. also *Lucrece*, 178, "dejected," 174, "dejection."

A. and V., 158, *prostrate*, in a very uncommon metaphorical usage:

Your daughter . . . most humbly

Prostrates her filial duty.

This is paralleled twice in Heywood's *The Rape of Lucrece*, and once in another play:

Rape of Lucrece, 173:

This hand . . .

Lays his victorious sword at Tarquin's feet,

And *prostrates* with that sword allegiance.

Pp. 211, 212:

The richest entertainment lives with us (*i.e.* that lives with us)

According to the hour, and the provision
Of a poor wife in the absence of her husband,
We *prostrate* to you.
Royal King and Loyal Subject, 42:
    To you . . . my liege,
A virgin's love I *prostrate*.
A. and. V, 153:
An *infinite*
Of fair Rome's sons.

"Infinite" is sometimes, though rarely, used by itself, more or less as a number. But used merely as a substantive, as here, it is very unusual. It is found in Heywood's *Rape of Lucrece*, 234, *Golden Age*, 36; cf. also *Rape of Lucrece*, 243:

Before thee *infinite* gaze on thy face.
A. and V., 153:
The iron wall
That rings this pomp in from *invasive* steel.

A rare word. Once in Shakespeare. The phrase is repeated in Heywood's *Golden Age*, 40:

The big Titanoys
Plow up thy land with their *invasive* steel.
A. and V., 153:
Let Janus' temple be *devolv'd* (*i.e.*overturned).

A very rare word in this sense. The *N.E.D.* gives only two other examples, one of 1470, one of 1658. Not in

Shakespeare. Heywood, *Lucrece*, 244:

For they behind him will *devolve* the bridge.

A. and V., 155:

You *mediate* excuse for courtesies.

(*i.e.* beg on somebody else's behalf.)

Rare: not in Shakespeare. In Webster's *The White Devil* in the sense of "to take a moderate position!" Marlowe and one or two prose-writers have used it in the sense of the text. It is found in Heywood, *English Traveller*, 84:

Will you. . . .

Not *mediate* my peace?

A. and V., 161:

Upon my *infallid* evidence.

Very rare: not in Shakespeare. *N.E.D.* gives only two other examples, of which one is Heywood, *Hierarch.*, v. 308:

All these are *infallid* testimonies.

A. and V., 174:

Let him come *thrill* his partisan

Against this breast.

"*Thrill*, i.e. hurl,—an unusual sense of the word," says Dyce. He adds two quotations, both from Heywood's *Iron Age*, e.g. p. 316:

All which their javelins *thrild* against thy breast.

Note the correspondence of phrase. This use is not found in Shakespeare.

A. and V., 174:

Marshal yourselves, and entertain this *novel* Within a ring of steel.

An uncommon substantive, not found in Shakespeare. Heywood, *English Traveller*, 27, *Golden Age*, 55, *Iron Age, Second Part*, 373, *Brazen Age*, 202.

A. and V., 178:

One reared on a popular suffrage
Whose station's built on *aves* and applause.

For this sense, "shouts of applause," the *N.E.D.* gives only two examples; one from Shakespeare (*Measure for Measure*) the other from Heywood, *Golden Age*, 8.

And all the people with loud suffrages
Have shrilled their *aves* high above the clouds.

Note the conjunction with "suffrage." The human brain works half mechanically along tiny associative paths; and minute hints of this kind, as a backing to more tangible instances of the uses of very rare words, importantly help this sort of proof. Heywood also uses the word uniquely, *Golden Age*, 47.

The people *ave'd* thee to heaven.

A. and V., 179:

This slight has stiffened all my *operant* powers.

Dyce quotes *Hamlet*, iii. 2:

My *operant* powers their function leave to do.

And it is quite probable that the author of *Appius and Virginia* is borrowing the phrase from Shakespeare, for the word is very uncommon. Heywood, in *The Royal King and the Loyal Subject*, probably written just about the same time as *Hamlet*, uses the word, in the same sense (p. 6), only writing "parts" instead of "powers." The sense of this passage is even nearer to the *Hamlet* line: they are obviously connected— through Heywood, as usual, echoing rather than imitating Shakespeare.

> When I forget thee may my *operant parts*
> Each one forget their office.

It seems to me probable that Heywood echoed Shakespeare immediately in *The Royal King and the Loyal Subject*, and soon after, rather less closely in *Appius and Virginia*.

A. and V., 179: *Strage*.

A rare Latinism: not in Shakespeare. Heywood uses it in *Pleasant Dialogues*, iii. and in *The Hierarchie*.[1]

There are other general verbal resemblances. The kind of word Heywood invents and uses is the same in *Appius and Virginia* and through the six volumes of his collected "dramatic works." "Eternized," "monarchizer," "applausive," "opposure" occur in the latter; "imposturous," "enthronized," "donative," in the former. Who could distinguish? In *Appius and Virginia*, 178, he invents (possibly adopts) the rare verb "to oratorize." In *The English Traveller*, 68, he uses the form "to orator." Resemblances of phrase are as numerous, though not so striking. Heywood was too ordinary and too hurried a writer to have much eccentricity of phrase. He wrote in the common style of the time, only slightly garnished by a few queer pet words and a certain Latinism of vocabulary. He does not repeat lines and metaphors as many writers do; only, occasionally, phrases and collocations of words, but these of such a kind as all his contemporaries repeated also. The result is that it is difficult to find parallels of this nature between any of his works. What there are between *Appius and Virginia* and the rest, therefore, have more weight than they would have in the case of some other dramatists.

There is a rather puzzling expression just at the end of *Appius and Virginia* (p. 180):

Appius died like a Roman gentleman,
And a man both ways knowing.

It is, metrically and in a sense, very like a sentence at the end of *The English Traveller* (p. 94):

Dalavill
Hath played the villain, but for Geraldine,
He hath been each way noble.

Cf. also *Fortune by Land and Sea*, 386:

Come! I am both ways armed against thy steel.

One of the few points which the author of *Appius and Virginia* introduced into the stories of Dionysius and Livy, is the plot to coerce Virginia by refusing the army's pay and forcing Virginius to sell his goods to pay them. In the first act of *A Maidenhood Well Lost* (espec. iii ff.) Strozza lays much the same plot against "the General" and his daughter, and what ensues, the army starving and the general paying the soldiers himself, is exactly the same. This shows, at least, that the idea was in Heywood's mind when he was writing *A Maidenhood Well Lost*. What is more significant is that another idea in the camp-scenes in *Appius and Virginia* (also original) was in his mind when he was writing *The Rape of Lucrece*. On page 205 the sentry makes the entirely unnecessary remark about his occupation:

Thus must poor soldiers do;

While their commanders are with dainties fed, And sleep on down, the earth must be our bed.

This is the *motif* of the whole mutiny-scene in *Appius and Virginia* (p. 156). See especially the lines:

I wake in the wet trench,

    Loaded with more cold iron than a gaol

    Would give a murderer, while the general

    Sleeps in a field-bed, and to mock our hunger

    Feeds us with scent of the most curious fare

    That makes his tables crack.

It is obvious that Heywood's mind ran easily into the same trains of thought. Suggest "Camp" to him, and he readily

169

pictures, in his pleasant light water-colours, the starving, cold soldiers *sub divo* and the general feeding luxuriously and enjoying a bed. Indeed, the parallels of idea with *Lucrece* are numerous, as one would expect. Heywood felt that a great man of that time was attended by a "secretary." Porsenna, King of the Tuscans, in his tent (*Lucrece*, 245) wants lights. He calls "Our Secretary!" The secretary appears with "My lord?" In *Appius and Virginia* (159, 160) when Appius is bearded by Icilius, he calls out for help, "Our secretary!" and summons him again at the end of the interview, "Our Secretary! . . . We have use for him." Marcus appears:

My honourable lord? . . .

There are other such small points—the bearing of the dead, bleeding bodies of Lucrece, and of Virginia, before the people, and their sympathy and rage; the vagueness of locality in each play; and so on.

But there is a more remarkable resemblance. It is part of a general link with Heywood's works—the clown. Dr Stoll has three pages (197—200) pointing out and illustrating the kinship of Corbulo in *Appius and Virginia* with Heywood's clowns, and especially the clown of *The Rape of Lucrece*.[1] The Heywood clown, an early type, was a simple, good-hearted creature, who had little to do with the play, and poured out puns and somewhat Euphuistic jokes to amuse the crowd. There was a painstaking, verbal tumbling they all indulged in. You can pick at random. "If they suddenly do not strike up," says Slime of the lingering musicians,[2] "I shall presently strike them[3] down." It is the voice of Corbulo. The clown in *The Golden Age* is precisely the same. So is the one in *Lucrece*, and as the plays are more alike, the similarity of his position is the more easily seen. It is, in the first place remarkable coincidence that he should be there at all. *Appius and Virginia* and *The Rape of Lucrece* are the only Roman plays of the adult Elizabethan drama to introduce such a character. It was exactly like Heywood to modify the tradition and *genus* in this way. It would not have been at all like Webster. Dr Stoll emphasises and details this similarity so admirably, and as he has no idea that *Appius and Virginia* is not by Webster, his testimony is so valuable in its impartiality, that I cannot do better than quote his description.

In both cases the clown is servant to the heroine, and he appears in like situations. He is sent by his mistress on errands, is taken to task by her for ogling at her maid (and that in the latter's presence), and is left to chatter with other servants alone. He jokes about his mistress's misfortune, about the sinners in the suburbs, and, being a Roman, out of the Latin grammar. And the comic side of both is the same. It lies all in the speeches—the clown plays no pranks and suffers no mishaps—and it has an episodic, random, and anachronistic character. It is all jest and repartee, puns, quibbles, and catches, and those neither clever nor new; and the drift of it all, whenever it gets beyond words, is satire on London life and manners. It is good-humoured moreover, naive and dirty.

The episode between the maid, or nurse, and the clown, an entirely irrelevant excrescence, is especially noteworthy. There is even a certain similarity in phrasing and thought, of a kind that suggests the same mind working at different times, rather than imitation. Virginia and Lucrece both address the clown as "Sir," impatiently. Virginia begins:

You are grown wondrous *amorous* of late;
Why do you look back so often?

LUCRECE. Sirrah, I ha' seen you oft familiar

With this my maid and waiting-gentlewoman,

As casting *amorous* glances, wanton looks,

And privy becks, savouring incontinence.

Dr Stoll, supposing *Appius and Virginia* Webster's, can of course only suggest that Webster, imitating Shakespeare in the general conception of his play, turned suddenly, picked out one favourite character of Heywood's, and, with Heywood's authority for the anachronism, introduced an extraordinarily good imitation of it into his own work. He is like a ventriloquist who has at least two lay-figures, each talking with a different voice from the other's, and from their master's. "Eclecticism" is a mild word for such a method.

172

IV

Anyone who believes in Webster's authorship of the play, has now got to explain away not only the date difficulty, not only the general æsthetic absurdity, not only the borrowing of a pet character of Heywood's, but also the sudden entire adoption of Heywood's individual, distinguishing vocabulary. Twenty years' friendship, you are to suppose, never affected Webster's vocabulary in this direction in the slightest degree. Then, in a transport of "senile" affection, he hurled aside his own personality, and became mere Tom.

In the next place, consider how the theory of Heywood's authorship suits the facts of the play. If Heywood wrote *Appius and Virginia*, there is no difficulty about words or handling. He wrote the play most like it of all the plays in the world. There is no difficulty about style. It is exactly like Heywood when he is writing solemnly, as in parts of *Lucrece*, parts of the various "Ages," and the beginning and end of *The Royal King and the Loyal Subject*. Only it is rather more mature, it has a little more freedom and rhetoric, than the early style of *Lucrece* and some of the "Ages." This suits the other indications of date. For, again, there is no difficulty about the date. The difference between *Lucrece* and *Appius and Virginia* is mostly due to the fact that *Corioianus* (*c.* 1608) must have intervened. Any date after 1608 would do;

immediately after is the most likely, because the resemblances of style and vocabulary are, on the whole, to the rather earlier works.

I imagine that the main part of *Appius and Virginia*, as we have it, was written then. It may, and indeed must, have been cut about and altered, by Heywood or others, before it found a last home with "Beeston's boys" in 1639, or a final resting-place with Moseley in 1654.

The metrical characteristics noticed in *Appius and Virginia* are Heywood's. Heywood's blank verse, says Dr Schipper,[1] is "sehr gewandt und harmonisch gebaut." This applies perfectly to our play. He also calls attention, of course, to the number of rhyming couplets, ending off even short speeches. It is this characteristic in *Appius and Virginia* that slightly puzzles Dr Stoll and suddenly upsets his metrical tables (p. 190). The only detailed examination of Heywood's prosody that I know is in Dr Franz Albert's "Über Thomas Heywood's *Life and Death of Hector of Troy*."[1] It is concerned mainly with certain sides of Heywood's work, mostly undramatic, and it is not very perspicacious, having most of the faults of Germans trying to understand English metre. But it enumerates some of the mare tangible characteristics, and lays great stress on that trick of conscious and rather conventionalised elision, especially between "to" and a verb with an initial vowel, that I had already independently noticed in *Appius and Virginia*, and have remarked on earlier in this appendix.

The various characteristics of the play that are no bar to Webster's authorship fit in equally well or better with Heywood's. This is the case with the numerous slight imitations of phrases of Shakespeare, which are rather more a mark of Heywood than of Webster.[2]

The sources of *Appius and Virginia*[3] are, ultimately, Livy and Dionysius of Halicarnassus. Dr Lauschke believes he used both of these, and also Painter, who paraphrased Livy, and Giovanni Fiorentino, the Italian translator of Dionysius. As Dr Stoll points out, there is no evidence for Giovanni Fiorentino, and very little for Livy in the original, as against Painter.[1] They do not seem, however, to have considered the possibility of Philemon Holland's well-known translation of Livy (1600). In the passage where the question of Virginia's custody till the trial is being discussed, Holland introduces the technical legal word "forthcoming." *Appius and Virginia* makes good use of the word in the corresponding passage (p. 167). Painter does not use it, and the Latin does not necessarily suggest it. The author of *Appius and Virginia* may have thought of it for himself, in reading the original. But it decidedly points to Holland being used; and therefore does away with the necessity of either Painter or Livy. It is certain that Dionysius was used,[2] in the original or a Latin translation (there was probably no English translation at this time). The sources, then, favour Heywood if anything. Of Webster's classical knowledge we can only say that he knew other people's Latin quotations. Thomas Heywood, Fellow of Peterhouse, translator of Sallust, Ovid, and Lucian, author of the learned *Hierarchie, Apology for Actors,* Γυναικ Ἐῖον, etc., was a lover of learning and a reader of Latin and Greek all his life.

V

It remains to see what explanation, on the assumption that Heywood is mainly or entirely the author of *Appius and Virginia*, can be given of the exiguous pieces of evidence that point towards Webster. There is first Moseley's attribution. I have said how little weight the attribution of a late publisher carries. In this case it is impossible to do much more than theorise about what can have happened. If Heywood's name was on the play when Moseley got it, it is unlikely he would have changed it for Webster's, not only because he seems to have been fairly honest, but also because there was not sufficient inducement. Of the two, however, Webster was the more famous and attractive after the Civil War. Winstanley (1686) (who—it is an odd accident— mentions all Webster's plays except *Appius and Virginia*) makes little of either of them. Phillips (1674) says Webster was the author of "several not wholly to be rejected plays"; on the identity of which, however, he was terribly shaky. Heywood he dismisses even more cursorily as the writer of "many but vulgar comedies." Langbaine, who always takes a rather high tone, describes Webster as "an author that lived in the reign of King James the First, and was in those days accounted an excellent poet." But he goes on to confess that *The Duchess of Malfi, The White Devil*, and *Appius and Virginia*, "have, even in our own age, gained applause." It was true. *The White Devil* was being acted at the Theatre Royal in 1671, and a quarto of it was printed in the following year. *The Duchess of Malfi* was acted in 1664 at Lincoln's Inn Fields, and in 1667 at the Duke's Theatre. It was reprinted in the same year. Downes (*Roscius Anglicanus*) describes it as "one of the best stock-tragedies." *Appius and Virginia*, as Webster's, with Betterton's alterations, was acted at the Duke's Theatre in 1670. Mrs Betterton was Virginia. Genest quotes from Downes that it ran for eight days, and was very frequently acted afterwards. All this shows that Webster's name was fairly well known in this period. There is no trace of any known play of Heywood's being revived.

It is easy enough to imagine a play of his coming without a name, or with a wrong name, into the hands of a publisher of 1654. There were two hundred and twenty plays "in which I have had either an entire hand or at least a main finger."[1] On any that came to the press in his lifetime, he seems to have kept an eye. For the others, when they had passed out of his control, he seems not to have cared. "Many of them, by shifting and change of companies have been negligently lost; others of them are still retained in the hands of some actors who think it against their peculiar profit to have them come in print."[2] *Appius and Virginia* may have belonged to either, more probably to the latter class. And it is very easy to trace a possible and probable history of this play.[1] We first hear of it in 1639, in the possession of Christopher Beeston's company of boys, who occupied the Cockpit Theatre from 1637 onwards. Now Christopher Beeston and Thomas Heywood were members of Queen Anne's company from its foundation in 1603. In 1617 the Cockpit opened, and Queen Anne's company went there till 1619. From 1619 to 1625 the lady Elizabeth's company held the Cockpit, and probably, though not certainly, Heywood and Beeston were of them. From 1625 to 1637 they were followed by Queen Henrietta's company, managed by Beeston. And then came Beeston's company of boys, who possessed the play in 1639. Among all the various strands of continuity in the Elizabethan theatres and companies, this is a very definite one, forming about Heywood and Beeston, in connection first with Queen Anne's company, and then, locally, with the Cockpit. And with Heywood, Beeston, and, I believe, *Appius and Virginia*, on this long journey, goes significantly *The Rape of Lucrece*.

It is also to be noticed that it was Queen Anne's company that acted two of Webster's three original plays, *The White Devil* (1611) and *The Devil's Law-Case* (1620). He seems to have gone off to the King's Men between these, with *The Duchess of Malfi* (1612-1613). But we may suppose that he had most to do with Queen Anne's company.

There remain the similarities and repetitions of phrase in *Appius and Virginia* and Webster's plays. As I have said, only three of these are of any importance, two exact verbal repetitions and one striking similarity of phrase and idea; all connecting with *The Duchess of Malfi*.[1] If Heywood wrote the main part or all of *Appius and Virginia*, there are six possible explanations of these passages. They are an accident; or Heywood imitated Webster; or Webster imitated Heywood; or the play was touched up by some Queen's company actor or author who knew *The Duchess of Malfi*; or Webster himself touched it up; or Webster and Heywood wrote *Appius and Virginia* together, Heywood taking the chief part.

The first is improbable, though far less improbable than it seems. For both (*a*) and (*g*) are sententious sayings such as the Elizabethans delighted to note down and repeat. Webster is full of these. And the identical repetition of one of them by him and Marston supported great theories of his imitation of Marston till Mr Crawford discovered it in Montaigne,[2] the common source to which they had independently gone.

Still, the coincidence of the two apophthegms is rather much to account for in this way. It is possible, but that is all. And there is the further difficulty against it that Heywood was not wont to write in this note-book manner. He worked too quickly.

This also counts against what might otherwise seem an easier theory, that (*f*) is either an accident or the imitation of reminiscence, but that these two (*a*) and (*g*) are the result of Heywood directly copying Webster—noting down and using two of his phrases. The possibility of this is also lessened by the probability on other grounds that *Appius and Virginia* is earlier than *The Duchess of Malfi*. Webster may have imitated Heywood. He was a great friend of his at this time.[1] And if *Appius and Virginia* was, as is probable, written early, it must have appeared in the same theatre and about the same time as *The White Devil*.[2] Also it was Webster's habit to take down from other authors and afterwards use sentences and similes of an apophthegmatic or striking nature. We know that he treated Donne, Montaigne, Jonson, Sidney, and perhaps Marston and Dekker in this way. Why not Heywood, his friend and collaborator? It is true Heywood does not lend himself often so easily to such use. That, and the fact that he has not been thoroughly searched for such a purpose, may explain why there are few other known parallels. This theory is the more probable because the lines of (*a*) and (*g*), and their ideas, seem more natural and in place in *Appius and Virginia* than they do in *The Duchess of Malfi*. And it is easier to imagine Webster finding (*Appius and Virginia*, 149),

I have seen children oft eat sweetmeats thus,
As fearful to devour them,

and adding (*Duchess of Malfi*, 65) the words "too soon " than Heywood doing the opposite.

There remain the various possibilities of two hands having been at work, or the same hand at two periods. These are favoured by the *a priori* probability of a play that had at least thirty years of acting life being altered in the period, and also by certain indications that all is not right with the play as it stands. These I shall shortly set out.

In the beginning of Act I. there is a queer and solitary passage of prose which looks like an abbreviation for acting purposes. Dyce suspects it; and it is to be noted that the speech following the prose contains one of the two "repetitions " from *The Duchess of Malfi*.

In II. 3 (p. 160) there are difficulties which seem to have passed unnoticed. Icilius comes to plead with Appius for the camp, and so for Virginius. Appius counters with a proposal that Icilius should give up Virginia, and marry into his own family. Icilius flies out with the charge that Appius has been lustfully tempting Virginia with presents and letters. Appius is prevented by force and threats from either calling for help or replying. At length the storm subsides. Appius replies, pretending he knows nothing of it, playing indulgent eld. Icilius crumbles completely.

I. I crave your pardon.

A. Granted ere craved, my good Icilius.

I. Morrow.

 A. It is no more indeed. Morrow, Icilius,

 If any of our servants wait without,

 Command them in.

I do not think any good sense can be made out of that "It is no more indeed." It looks, at first sight, like a pun on "morrow." But that does not help, Indeed the whole collapse of Icilius is oddly curt and sudden. It seems to me probable that a cut has been made here, or some other operation of hasty revision.

And in the next scene, III. 1 (pp. 161-2) Icilius reports the interview to his friends and Virginia. He went, he says, to Appius, took him by the throat, forced him to hear, taxed him with his lust and his behaviour, "with such known circumstance" that Appius could try to excuse it, but could not deny it. They parted "friends in outward show"; Appius swore "quite to abjure her love"; but yet had continued his messages.

Now this is quite a different story from the truth. In a play of this kind, simple in characterisation and full of childishness in construction and episode, we cannot suppose the author was attempting the subtle irony Ibsen practised in *The Wild Duck*, where you see the truth in one scene and Hialmar Ekdal's family version of it in the next. Nor would such a sudden spasm of Euripidean double-dealing help either the character of Icilius or the play. Besides, there are other indications of confusion. For when (III. 2, p. 164) Virginia is suddenly arrested, she cries out:

> O my Icilius, your incredulity
> Hath quite undone me!

which seems to refer to the *first*, true version of the story, and to mean that Icilius' not believing her but accepting Appius' defence had ruined her. These seem to me to be plain signs that the scenes as they stand have been written, to some extent at least, by two people, or by the same person at different times.

Another discrepancy affecting the same point, the interview and the report of it, is mentioned by Dyce in his note on II. 3 (p. 158). The scene would seem to be an outer apartment in the house of Appius. But presently, when Appius is left alone with Icilius, a change of scene is *supposed:* for he says to Claudius (p. 160):

> To send a ruffian hither,
> Even to my closet!

And yet, in the first scene of the next act, Icilius speaks of the interview as having taken place in the lobby!

The only other suspicion of corruption in this play which I know of may as well be mentioned here. Mr Pierce[1] believes that III. 4, the conversation between Corbulo and the serving-men, was interpolated to please the groundlings. His reasons are: (1) it is wholly in prose; (2) the doggerel rhyme; (3) it does not advance the action; (4) the average number of three-syllable Latin words (his particular test) is very low. I do not feel convinced. The scene is extremely Heywoodian. The Latin-word test is not so important as Mr Pierce appears to think, especially when applied to a short, rather comic, prose-scene. And it affects Heywood far less than Webster. No doubt this scene was put in "to please the groundlings." But it was put in by the author.

The conclusion, then, that the play as we have it has been revised and altered, helps any theory that Webster and Heywood each had a finger in it. It might, of course, have been changed by any member of the Queen's Servants' Company. But he would not be likely to have incorporated passages from *The Duchess of Malfi*, a play belonging to the King's Men. If it was Heywood himself that touched it up, in 1613 or so, he might quite well have done this, being a friend of Webster's. But it is most easy to suppose Webster the reviser. Either this, or his collaboration, is rendered rather probable by the presence through the play of ten or a dozen passages, averaging perhaps two lines, that seem to taste slightly of his style. Perhaps it is true that any play, examined closely, would yield the same. And certainly Heywood *could* have written them. But, at moments, there does seem to be the flavour, almost imperceptibly present. If reviser or collaborator, Webster obviously had recourse to the same note-books as he used for *The Duchess of Malfi*, which suggests that he would be working on it about 1612 or soon after. And in either case, we should have a very good explanation of his name being connected with the play. If he revised, we must suppose that he shortened and made more dramatic the very beginning of the play, and heightened, or even rewrote, the trial scene (IV. 1). It is important to notice that in this rather long scene (1) there are no very characteristic words of Heywood's, (2) there are more of the phrases, words and lines that are faintly reminiscent of Webster than anywhere else in the play,[1] (3) two[2] of the three strong indications of a connection with Webster occur.

Give Webster the revision of these two scenes, and you have satisfied his utmost claims. To yield him more is mere charity. If he collaborated, it is impossible to divide the play up between the two. In certain scenes (*e.g.* IV. 2 and V. 3) Heywood's vocabulary comes out more clearly than in the rest. But one can only say that Webster's part is very small compared with Heywood's, as unimportant as it is in

Northward Ho and *Westward Ho*.

In sum: general, critical, and æsthetic impressions, more particular examination of various aspects, and the difficulty of fitting it in chronologically, make it impossible to believe that *Appius and Virginia* is by Webster, while the evidence in favour of his authorship is very slight. All these considerations, and also remarkable features of vocabulary and characterisation, make it highly probable that it is by Heywood. The slight similarities between *The Duchess of Malfi* and *Appius and Virginia* may be due to Webster borrowing in *The Duchess of Malfi* from Heywood, or revising *Appius and Virginia*, or having, not for the first time, collaborated with Heywood, but very subordinately. In any case, *Appius and Virginia* must be counted among Heywood's plays; not the best of them, but among the better ones; a typical example of him in his finer moments, written rather more carefully than is usual with that happy man.

[1] The only other *Appius and Virginia* known is the old-fashioned lumbering play by "R. B." (probably Riohard Bower) of 1576.

[2] C.H.E.L., vol. vi. p. 182.

[1] *E.g. Duchess of Malfi*, III. 2:

"Did you ever in your life know an ill painter
Desire to have his dwelling next door to the shop
Of an excellent picture maker?"

² For the perplexing metrical part which *Appius and Virginia* plays, see the metrical table on p. 190 of Dr Stoll's *John Webster*. Its resembalance to *A Cure for a Cuckold* is only in some directions, and more statistioal than real. The metre of both is rather smooth; but in a very different way. It is, of course, rather risky to lay much emphasis on *A Cure for a Cuckold*: it may have been worked over by Rowley.

¹ See page 200.

¹ *E.g.* "To obey, my lord, and to know how to rule . . ."

² Stoll, pp. 193-197, illustrates this fully enough. A single reading of the play will prove it.

¹ For Moseley and his activities, *v. Dictionary of National Biography*; Plomer, *Dictionary of Booksellers and Printers*, 1641-1667; Masson, *Life of Milton*, iii. 448-457, vi. 352; Parrott, *Tragedies of Chapman*, p. 683; Malone, *Variorum Shakespeare*, iii. 229.

¹ The references are all by the pages of Dyce's one-volume edition.

¹ Quarto reading. Dyce reads "matchless": obviously wrongly.

¹ So Quarto. Dyce thinks this a mistake for "The office of justice. . . .– as in *The Duchess of Malfi* quotation. He is probably right.

¹ Especially the similarity between "in a mist," *A. and V.*, 167, and "in a mist," *White Devil*, 50.

[1] The references to Heywood's plays are to the pages of the six-volume Pearson edition, 1874.

[1] The earlier and longer form of this appendix contains about a dozen further instances of verbal similarity, which were omitted in the later version as being rather less striking than those given here, and therefore unnecessary to the argument.

[1] See also Eckhardt, *Die lustige Person im älteren englischen Drama*, p. 433, etc.

[2] *A Woman killed with Kindness*, 97.

[3] Old Text "thee!"

[1] *Englische Metrik*, 1881, vol. ii. p. 335

[1] Especially pp. 22, 172.

[2] See *Cambridge History of English Literature*, vol. vi. p. 106.

[3] See Lauschke, "John Webster's Tragödie *Appius and Virginia*," and Stoll, pp. 160-162.

[1] There are two points: (*a*) Livy has "sordidatus"; *A.* and *V.* "disguised in dust and sweat"; Painter nothing. This is very little, and becomes nothing when you realise—Dr Stoll does not point it out, though Lauschke does—that "sordidatus" and "disguised . . ." come in entirely different parts of the story. (*b*) Minutius as the name of the general at Algidum occurs in Livy, not in Painter or Dionysius. This has a little weight.

² *V.* Stoll, p. 162, for conclusive proofs.

¹ *The English Traveller:* To the Reader.

²*Ibid.*

¹ See Murray, *English Dramatic Campanies*, vol. i. pp. 265-270, and elsewhere.

¹ (*a*), (*f*), and (*g*) in my list (pp. 175-177).

² Crawford, *Collecianea*, Series ii. p. 35.

¹ He wrote some lines "To his beloved friend Master Thomas Heywood," prefixed to Heywood's *Apology for Actors*, 1612.

² It is an important indication of the date of *Appius and Virginia* that *The White Devil* (1611) does not borrow from it, and *The Duchess of Malfi* (1612-13) does.

¹ *The Collaboration of Webster and Dekker.*

¹ "Dunghill," "mist," "pursenet," "to bring my girl asleep," "and this short dance of life is full of changes," etc. etc.

² *I.e.* (*f*) and (*g*).

APPENDIX B.—MISCELLANEOUS

NON-EXTANT PLAYS

There are no difficulties about the dates of most of the non-extant plays. *Cæsar's Fall, Two Shapes*, and *Christmas Comes but Once a Year* are dated 1602 by the entries in Henslowe. Dr Greg from the list of collaborators and the nearness in date of the payments thinks *Cæsar's Fall* and *Two Shapes* must be the same play; it may be so, but it is not convincing. Henslowe may very well have been employing the same people in the same month to write two plays. There is a doubt about the name of *Two Shapes*. That is Dr Greg's reading. Collier read *Two Harpes*; which some construe *Two Harpies*.

A Late Murther of the Son upon the Mother by Ford and Webster is entered in Herbert's Office Book for September 1624. Pamphlets of July 1624 about such a murder case are on record. The play must have been written in that year.

The *Guise*, which Webster mentions in his Dedication

to *The Devil's Law-Case*, is of quite unknown date. An entry in Henslowe for 1601 giving Webster a play of that name turns out to be a forgery of Collier's. The orginal entry probably referred to Marlowe's *Massacre at Paris*. Dr Stoll, scenting Marlowe in Webster's latest plays, has spun a theory of Webster reading up Marlowe, especially the *Massacre at Paris*, in his old age. He deduces that we can date *Guise* about 1620. The whole theory rests on a quite wild assumption that an Elizabethan dramatist, wishing to write a play on a certain subject, began by reading up all previous plays on that subject, like a professor of English Literature. If Webster's own list of plays is in chronological order, *Guise* is later than 1614. We can say no more.

"THE THRACIAN WONDER"

The Thracian Wonder, like *A Cure for a Cuckold*, was first published in 1661 by Francis Kirkman as by Webster and Rowley. No one believes it to be by either. The reasons of this disbelief are entirely æsthetic. It is dangerous, as I have said elsewhere, to take it for granted that a bad play cannot be by a good author. It is conceivable that Webster and Rowley might have written or helped to write a play like this at the beginning of their careers. Each has been concerned in equally bad work. But if they did write it, it does not increase our knowledge of them; and if they did not write it, it does not matter who did. So the affair is not very important. A rather unsuccessful attempt has been made to explain Kirkman's attribution. Another Webster in 1617 wrote a story, which had no connection with this play, but which Kirkman may have thought had. It is not necessary. Kirkman was one of the wildest of the Restoration publishers. The fact that he was publishing one play as by Webster and Rowley might quite likely lead him to put their names on the title-page of its twin. Anyhow he has no authority. We do not know who did or who did not write *The Thracian Wonder*.

"MONUMENTS OF HONOUR"

Monuments of Honour is a quite ordinary city triumph, there is nothing remarkable or important about it. It was published in 1624 as by John Webster, merchant taylor. "John Webster" was a common enough name, and there is no proof that this one is our author. The Latin tag on the title-page, which also ends the preface to *The White Devil*, was in common use. There is only the probability that no other John Webster would have been distinguished enough in literature to have been chosen to write this. The guilds generally liked to get hold of some fairly accomplished literary man for such a purpose. Neither the verse nor the invention of this pageant affirms the authorship of Webster. But there is also nothing to contradict it.

APPENDIX C.—SIR THOMAS WYATT

"THE FAMOUS HISTORY OF SIR THOMAS WYATT."

Date.

The Famous History of Sir Thomas Wyatt. With the Coronation of Queen Mary and the Coming In of King Philip. Written by Thomas Dickers and John Webster, was printed in 1607.[1] In October 1602, Chettle, Dekker, Heywood, Smith, and Webster were paid, in all, £8 for Part I. of *Lady Jane or The Overthrow of Rebels*; and Dekker was paid, in earnest, 5s. for Part II. (Smith and Chettle may have received small amounts for this, also.) All this was on behalf of Worcester's Men, who passed under the patronage of Queen Anne in 1608. As the 1607 Quarto of *Sir Thomas Wyatt* says it was played by the Queen's Majesty's Servants, and as the authors are the same, there is no reason to doubt that Dyce was right in supposing that *Sir Thomas Wyatt* consists of fragments of both parts of *Lady Jane*. Dr Stoll thinks perhaps we have only Part I., as

The Coronation of Queen Mary and *The Coming In of King Philip* are only promised and not given. Dr Greg suggests that the cut version of Part I. ends and Part II. begins, with Mary's audience (p. 193, column 2; Scene 10). Professor Schelling makes the credible suggestion that the censor had cut out a great deal; especially, no doubt, the *Coming In of King Philip*. As it stands, the play is extraordinarily short. In any case, the date is 1602. It must have been played at "The Rose"; and, as there are two editions, it was probably revived.

Sources.

The source of *Sir Thomas Wyatt*—that is, of the two parts of *Lady Jane*—is Holinshed; and, as far as we know, nothing else.[1]

Collaboration.

Opinions have differed as to the respective amounts contributed by Dekker and Webster. Dr Stoll, arguing from metre, sentiment, style, phrases, and the general nature of the play, can find Dekker everywhere, Webster nowhere. Dr Greg gives Webster rather more than half, mostly the first half. Mr Pierce[2] says that Webster wrote "most of Scenes 2, 5, 6, 10, 14, and 16, although some of these scenes were certainly retouched by Dekker, and all of them may have been." I shall discuss Mr Pierce's method of assigning scenes more closely in the Appendix on *Westward Ho* and

Northward Ho. In the case of *Sir Thomas Wyatt* none of his metrical tests seems to me to have any validity. They depend, like Dr Stoll's, on the assumption that Webster's metrical characteristics were the same in 1602 as in 1610 or 1620— an assumption Mr Pierce himself confesses to be absurd. It must be recognised that we have only three plays on which we can base our generalisations about Webster's metre, two slowly-written Italian tragedies of about 1610 or 1612 and a tragi-comedy of 1620. In *Sir Thomas Wyatt* Webster was writing a different kind of play, together with a lot of other people, probably in a great hurry; and it is likely he was immature. To take the statistics for rhyme in *The Duchess of Malfi* and the other plays and use them, as proving that Webster uses rhyme less than Dekker, to apportion the scenes in *Sir Thomas Wyatt*, is a glaring example of that statistical blindness and inert stupidity that has continually spoilt the use of the very valuable metrical tables that have been prepared for Elizabethan Drama. The evidence that metre gives in *Sir Thomas Wyatt* can only be of the vaguest description.

So, too, with characters. The reason why there are certain kinds of character and incident in any of these three partnership plays, is not that Dekker wrote them. It is that they are that kind of play. If Webster wrote a citizen's-wife-gallant play, he must have introduced citizens' wives and gallants, even if he did not do so in an Italian tragedy. On page 2 of his book Mr Pierce claims that his study is useful as throwing light on Webster's range as an author. "If Webster wrote . . . the parts of Captain Jenkins and Hans Van Belch in *Northward Ho*, then he showed an element of pleasant humour and manysidedness which is not indicated anywhere else." In Chapter VII., dealing with "The Character and Atmosphere-Test," he quotes with approval, as proof of what is and what is not Dekker's, Dr Stoll on these characters. "Manifestly Dekker's too are the Dutch Drawer and Merchant, and the Welsh Captain. A Dutch Hans had already appeared in the *Shoemaker* . . . and Captain Jenkins . . . is the counterpart of Sir Vaughan ap Rees in *Satiro-Mastix*." That is to say, these characters of common types are Dekker's, because Dekker uses similar ones elsewhere, and not Webster's because Webster doesn't. You start out to see if Webster, having written only in a certain style elsewhere, wrote in another style here. You conclude that he has not written in this other style here, *because* he has written only in a certain style elsewhere!

Considerations of style (in the narrower sense of literary individuality) and vocabulary are more convincing. The only one of Mr Pierce's tests that has any value in the case of *Sir Thomas Wyatt*—except, of course, the parallel-passages, taken with caution—is his three-syllable-Latin-word one.[1] A large proportion of Latin words, and any other characteristic we recognise clearly as one of the later Webster's, do *tend* to prove his presence in a scene—though their absence does not disprove it. These slight indications of style, *if* they had arisen and become unconscious so early, are the things that would be apparent in plays of different species by the same author. But the eight or ten years, and the probable presence of so many authors in this play, must make us sceptical. The latter point, indeed, would falsify most of Mr Pierce's work if it were sound on other grounds. He remembers, on his last page, that Heywood, Chettle, and Smith also have to be accounted for. He dismisses them too magnificently. "It would be useless to discuss such questions as these at present, since no practical results could follow. We have offered such evidence as we possess on the shares of Dekker and Webster; and here we stop." But though you may not have "discussed" the question of the relative shares of C., D., and E., in a play, you have definitely answered it, if you say A. wrote six scenes and B. the rest. The Latin-word test is no good unless we have Heywood's, Chettle's, and Smith's figures, as well as Dekker's and Webster's. It does not prove that Dekker wrote certain scenes and Webster did not, to say that Dekker employs a "sweet personal tone," or a market-girl with her eggs, elsewhere, and Webster does not. You have to be able to say that Heywood and Chettle and Smith also are strangers to these things.

Miss Mary Leland Hunt, in her recent monograph on Dekker,[1] also discusses the question of the partition of this play. Her most original suggestion is that the main plan of the play is due to Chettle. She advances various indications of this; that he was older than Dekker (and Webster, no doubt); that Henslowe mentions his name first; that he was specially at home in the chronicle history; and that he is more old-fashioned—and so more likely to have planned the old-fashioned structure of *Sir Thomas Wyatt*—than Dekker. Against Dekker and Webster this certainly holds true; and, in the midst of our uncertainties, the conjecture may be allowed to stand as more persuasive than any alternative. Beyond this, Miss Hunt has not much of value to contribute. She hints a vague approval of Fleay's attribution of scenes 1-9 to Webster, 11-17 to Dekker. But she qualifies this by giving Dekker parts of 7 and 9, and probably 4, and Webster 10. The pathos of the trial-scene (16), she thinks, points to Dekker.

Her judgment is not very trustworthy. It is based on emotional rather than æsthetic grounds—she attributes, I mean, a tender scene to Dekker and a gloomy scene to Webster, because Dekker is a tender, and Webster a gloomy, dramatist.

Welcoming a suggestion of Dr Greg's, she finds the

speeches of Wyatt in 6 and 10 very un-Dekkerish, and therefore gives these scenes to Webster. (Mr Pierce, more "scientifically" notices the same thing.) For myself, speaking with all due mistrust of human ability to pick out one author from another in these cases, I thought I too found a different note in these scenes. But if it is not Dekker's, it is as certainly neither the Webster's of 1612 nor the "Webster's" of the fancied Websterian parts of this play. It seems to me far more probably Heywood.[1]

The whole position is this. *Sir Thomas Wyatt* consists of the fragments of the first or of both of two plays, one by Chettle, Dekker, Heywood, Smith, and Webster, the other certainly by Dekker, and probably by the others as well. It is issued as by Webster and Dekker—either because they originally had the larger share, or because they did the editing, or because their names were at the moment the more likely to secure a sale, or because they were known as the authors of the play to the publisher. In any case, it was not the custom to put more than two names to a play. On the whole, therefore, one must begin with an *a priori* probability that *most* of the play as we have it is by Webster and Dekker, but that *some* is by Heywood or Smith or Chettle. In addition, the state of the play (the text is very uneven, sometimes fairly good, sometimes terribly mangled), and its history of slashing and patching, make it likely that the different contributions are fairly well mixed together by now. In some places, certainly, a delicate reader will fancy he detects repeated swift changes between more than two styles.[1]

It is obvious, then, that it is very presumptuous to assign different portions of the play with any completeness to the different authors. Reading the play, with careful attention to style and atmosphere, I have seemed to myself to recognise in the bulk of two scenes and in one or two scattered places (*e.g.* the opening lines of the play) a voice that may well be that of the younger Webster. Taking, therefore, cautiously a certain amount of positive evidence from Dr Stoll and Mr Pierce, and comparing it with my own impression of the play and the general impression of other critics, I suggest the following conclusions as all that we can fairly pretend to be more than amiable dreaming. Webster probably wrote scene 2 and most of scene 16. No doubt he poured indistinguishably forth other parts of this commonplace bit of journalism; but, except one or two lines, it is impossible to pick them out. A good deal of the rest of the play is by Dekker. Heywood's hand is occasionally to be suspected.

[1] *V.* Greg. Henslowe's Diary, Pt. ii. pp. 232, 3. There was another edition in 1612.

[1] *V.* Stoll, p. 45.

[2] *The collaboration of Webster and Dekker.* I use his division into scenes, which is the same as Fleay's.

[1] See the Appendix on *Westward Ho* and *Northward Ho*

[1] *Thomas Dekker: A Study*, by Mary Leland Hunt.

[1] Note especially the word "ostend," p. 194.

[1] *e.g.* the change towards the end of scene 11, at the top of page 196, after Suffolk's entry.

APPENDIX D.—"WESTWARD HO" AND

"NORTHWARD HO"

These plays are so closely connected, and evidence about either reacts so much on the other, that it is convenient to consider them together.

Dates.

They can be dated fairly closely.

Westward Ho was registered to print on March 2nd, 1605. It was printed in 1607.

Northward Ho was registered on August 6th, 1607, and printed in that year.

Northward Ho contains an amiable farcical attack on Chapman.[1] For this reason and others, it must have been written as an answer to *Eastward Ho*, which was registered to print September 4th, 1605, and appeared in several editions in that year, and was probably written in 1604, perhaps in 1605.[2] *Eastward Ho* was written, again, more or less in emulous succession to *Westward Ho*.[1] So we have the order of the plays fairly certain. Dekker and Webster wrote theirs for the Children of Paul's; *Eastward Ho* was written for the rival company, the children of the Queen's Revels, by Chapman, with the help of Jonson and Marston.

Westward Ho, therefore, could have been written any time before March 1605. The probable date of *Eastward Ho* makes it slightly desirable to put the performance of *Westward Ho* back, at least, towards the beginning of 1604. There are various references; to Kemp's London to Norwich Dance (1600);[2] perhaps to James' Scotch Knights;[3] and to the famous siege of Ostend.[4] Ostend was taken in September 1604, and the second quotation, at least, looks as if it was written after that. It may, however, have been written during the last part of the siege. And these references may, of course, not be of the same date as the rest of the play. But it seems fairly safe to date it as 1608[5] or 1604, with a slight preference for the autumn of 1604.[6]

Northward Ho, then, must have been written in 1605, 1606, or 1607. In Day's *The Isle of Gulls* (printed 1606) there seems to be a reference to these three plays,[1] in a passage that must have been written for a first performance; which cuts out, at least, 1607, and the last part of 1606. Dr Stoll records also[2] a close parallel with a passage in Marston's *The Fawn*. He thinks *The Fawn* is the originator, and that it was written in 1606.[3] But he dates it by a very uncertain reference to an execution. It is generally dated earlier, and Marston *may* have imitated *Northward Ho*, or the passages may, as in another Marston-Webster case, have been taken independently otherwhence. So the safest date for *Northward Ho* is 1605.[4]

Sources.

Westward Ho and *Northward Ho* are ordinary citizen-comedies. The sources of these are generally unknown. The plots were probably invented or adapted from some current event or anecdote. As Mr Arnold Bennett says (thinking of such bourgeois subjects as these plays deal with), there is no difficulty about a plot; you can get a plot any time by going into the nearest bar and getting into conversation over a drink. The Elizabethans, no doubt, did this. All that was wanted was some intrigue on the old citizen's-wives-gallants theme that would allow of practical joking, bawdy talk, and a little broad conventional character-drawing. Dr Stoll[1] and Mr Pierce[2] have pointed out that various incidents in these plays have similarities in other plays of Dekker's earlier or later. The "borrowing" from *Sophonisba* I have dealt with. The ring story in *Northward Ho* is paralleled in Malespini's *Ducento Novelle*,[3] as Dr Stoll points out. It can be traced further back (to the detriment of Dr Stoll's suggestion that it originated in an exploit of some attendants on Cardinal Wolsey), to number sixty-two in La Sale's *Les Cent nouvelles*

Nouvelles, a collection of the middle of the fifteenth century.[4] From La Sale it could easily have come into any of the Elizabethan books of stories, directly or by degrees. Or it might even have been merely reinvented.

Collaboration.

Dr Stoll has given some pages, and Mr Pierce two-thirds of his book, to an elaborate attempt to divide up these plays between Dekker and Webster. It is not possible here to examine either their methods or their results in detail. I can only suggest some principles which should be kept in mind in attempting such questions, and which they have not always kept in mind, and summarise their results, indicating how far they seem valid and valuable. I shall mostly consider Mr Pierce's work, as it is later and far more detailed than Dr Stoll's and includes it.[1]

Dr Stoll finds that the general outline and spirit of the plays, the characters, and most of the incidents are repeated in Dekker's other city-plays. On these grounds, and on grounds of style and phrase, he gives Dekker, in a general way, the whole of the plays. Mr Pierce adopts a more systematic method. He employs various tests, "scientific" and "æsthetic," separately, and tabulates and compares the results. His tests are of the following kinds; parallel passages; use of dialect; metrical; incidents; "character and atmosphere;" and the "three-syllable Latin-word test," an invention of his own. The last needs explanation. Mr Pierce discovered that the difference in typical passages of Webster and Dekker, the difference of weight and rhythm, is partly due to the number of long Latin words used by the former. He has made this into a regular and usable test, by reducing all Webster's and Dekker's plays to a common line measure, and finding the percentage of three-syllable words of Latin or Greek origin, in each scene and act. An ingenious plan. The results are superficially of immense decision and value. Webster's known plays have a high average; Dekker's known plays a low one. A few scenes in these two collaborate plays have a high average, and the rest a low one. There is a wide, almost empty gap in between. The conclusion, especially if other tests agree, is obvious.

But this test makes certain assumptions which Mr Pierce does not seem to have considered. It assumes that the use of these three-syllable Latin words is always independent of the subject-matter. It assumes that it was, even at this date, not only a habit of Webster's, but an ingrained one, and probably unconscious. If (and it is very probable) he was merely forming his style at this time, by imitating such writers as Marston, he could and would drop this trick a good deal, or forget to keep it up, in writing this sort of play. Writers are not born polysyllabic. The habit may supremely suit them; but they acquire it. And the process of acquiring it is generally conscious. When Webster wrote (or copied out)

> "I remember nothing.
> There's nothing of so infinite vexation
> As man's own thoughts."

or

> "I have caught
> An everlasting cold: I have lost my voice
> Most irrecoverably."

he knew what he was doing as well as Mr Henry James does when he writes, "She just charmingly hunched her eyes at him."

If the investigators of the future draw up lists of the average number of adverbs to a uniform line in Mr Henry James' works, they will find, probably, that in the early works it is practically normal, in the early-middle period uneven, varying from chapter to chapter, and for the last twenty years immense. Who they will think wrote the early, and collaborated in the middle, Henry James's, it is impossible to guess.

That this Latinism could be put on at will we have Dekker's *The Gull's Horn-Book* and passages in his more serious plays to witness. In spite of that it may be admitted that a quite high average in any scene in *Northward Ho* or *Westward Ho*, where Dekker would have no temptation to Latinise, does point to

Webster. But what Mr Pierce does not seem to realise is that a low average does not point in the same way to Dekker. For as there is no play of this kind by Webster extant, it is impossible to say how much he might have descended from Latinity at times. It is all part of the general error of taking, as Webster's normal usages, his practices in a definite kind of play in his mature period. Still, with these restrictions and in this way, Mr Pierce's Latin-word test has a good deal of value; that is to say, for deciding what is Webster's, not what is not. The only thing that can be urged against it is that it is unnecessary; being only a symptom of a difference in style which a subtle taste should distinguish on its own qualities, or, if more, misleading. This is mostly true; and the æsthetic tests are ultimately the most valuable. But then it is so hard either to fix or to communicate them.

The tests of metre, incident, and character and atmosphere seem to me to have practically no value, except in so far as "atmosphere" means literary style. What it mainly means is the complexion of the whole, with regard to which *Westward Ho* is of course much nearer to, say, *The Honest Whore*, than it is to *The Duchess of Malfi*. No doubt there *are* minor, barely visible, effects and individualities of metre, phrase, or character-drawing, and turns of incident, which might easily betray the Dekker of this period, whom we know, or even the Webster, whom we fear we mightn't recognise. Dr Stoll, indeed, has used these a little, for distinguishing Webster. But as a rule these details are just those one cannot tabulate. The grosser ones, that can be defined and listed, are the attributes of the species of play, such as a dramatist can put on and off at will. The subtler, less extricable peculiarities, however, are what influence the "unscientific" critical taste to feel, "This is Webster!" and "This Dekker!" They have an ultimate voice in deciding attributions, though by a different method from metrical or word-tests; by representation rather than plebiscite.

The second trustworthy kind of evidence, then, for a passage or scene being by some author, is a perception that the literary and linguistic style is his. To use this, which Swinburne called judging by the ear instead of the fingers, is a very important method, if not so supreme as he thought. It is without rules; but in this case there are certain general features of style which can be mentioned, if not tabulated. For Dekker there is the half-comical, quick, repetition of phrases, that Dr Stoll has noticed. There is an important unobserved characteristic of Webster's, which is extremely noticeable in his later works, and seems to appear in those portions of these plays which, on stylistic and other grounds, we are led to believe his. It is in marked contrast to Dekker. It is the use of involved sentences with subordinate clauses, as against a style where the ideas are expressed in a series of simpler, shorter, co-ordinate sentences. *Northward Ho*, II. 2, one of the only certainly Websterian scenes in the two plays, strikes the ear immediately as different in this way. The whole ring of the sentences is—mainly for this reason— slower, deeper, more solemn. The Germans have invented a way of distinguishing collaborators. Read the play, they say, and you find your voice instinctively assumes a different pitch for the work of different authors. They profess to tell to half a sentence where Webster begins and Dekker leaves off. One can smile at their whole claim. But, for these two authors, it is not, essentially, unmeaning.

The third admissible way of dividing the authorship of these plays, is by parallel passages. It is not generally kept in mind that if this method is used for deciding between collaborators, it implies an assumption that the collaboration was of a certain kind, namely, by taking so many scenes each. This was the usual practice in contemporary collaboration, we know; and it is, obviously, far the quickest and easiest way, as a rule. So we have a right, generally, to suppose that collaboration was of this sort, and, therefore, that a certain parallel or repetition is strong proof of authorship of that scene. All the same, there is always the possibility of both authors working over the same scene, in which case, of course, a parallel helps to prove nothing except its own source. In the present case, though we do not know so certainly as with Webster's earlier plays, *Sir Thomas Wyatt* or *Christmas comes but once a year*, that the collaboration was real and contemporary, it is very likely. The likelihood is made smaller than usual by the facts that Dekker was a much quicker worker than Webster, and that he was by standing and experience the senior partner. He might very well have gone over Webster's scenes.

On the whole then a single parallel or repetition does not prove much, in these plays; a row of them, in one scene, goes far to establish the authorship of that scene.

Mr Pierce has collected a great number of possible parallels, most of them insignificant, some of them very valuable. In using them, one must remember that we have only a very few, and quite different, later plays by Webster to draw on, and a great many, some contemporary and similar, of Dekker's. Once again, absence of proof that a scene is Webster's does not prove it is not.

By these methods of proof, and any outstanding evidence of another kind, one reaches much the same conclusions as Mr Pierce; but, I think, they should be applied differently. In *Northward Ho*, II. 2, and the first part of V., are almost certainly in the main by Webster. In *Westward Ho* there is not, it seems to me, the same certainty. But I. 1 and III. 3 show very strong traces of his presence. With *Northward Ho*, I. 1 and III. 1 the probability is smaller, but still considerable.

There are also one or two phrases or sentences scattered about the plays that arrest one's attention as recognisably Webster's, or at least not Dekker's. But these do not extend their atmosphere beyond themselves. There are these few scenes, which, with varying degrees of probability, can be given to Webster. There are a few more (*Westward Ho*, II. 1, 2, V. 3: *Northward Ho*, IV. 1.) where all the evidence points to Dekker being mainly responsible. In the rest, while we cannot detect the Webster of 1612, we have no right to deny the presence of the Webster of 1605. In any case the collaboration seems to have been of an intricate and overlaid nature.

To pretend to more precise knowledge is, I think, silly.

Since I wrote this, Miss Hunt's book on Thomas Dekker has appeared. On pages 106, 107, and 108 she discusses the shares of Webster and Dekker in these plays. She principally follows Fleay, whose methods were rough. She discusses the responsibility for the plots, which other critics have been inclined to leave vaguely to Dekker. She would give most of it to Webster, and also "the more unusual subtle or abnormal incidents"; the device of the diamond in *Westward Ho* and that of the ring in *Northward Ho*, perhaps also Greeneshield's betrayal of his wife, although that may have been borrowed from *Eastward Ho*. Also Justiniano's disguise as a hag; and his and Mayberry's jealousy. Other kinds of evidence she does not consider. In *Westward Ho* she finds signs of incomplete collaboration and change of plan in construction. Still following Fleay she thinks Webster wrote most of Acts I., II., and III., and some of IV.; Dekker, the rest. *Northward Ho* is more homogeneous. Dekker is given the Chapman-ragging and the Doll scenes; Webster the rest. Dekker probably went over the whole.

Her proofs and judgments are very superficial, and almost valueless. It is, perhaps, probable that Webster had more share in the planning of the plots and incidents than he has been allowed. Her assignments in general are based on a feeling that these two plays are "gross," "offensive," and "sinning against the light," that her protégé Dekker, being a pure-minded man, can have had little to do with them, and that Webster "who dealt with lust" must be held guilty. Her sex, or her nationality, or both, have caused in her a curious agitation of mind whenever she approaches these plays. This prejudice destroys what little value her very cursory investigation of the problems of their authorship might otherwise have had.

[1] This is fairly conclusively proved by Stroll (pp. 65-69). The only doubtful point is that Bellamont (whom we suppose to mean Chapmen) is called "white" and "hoary." Chapman was only forty-seven in 1606. But even in this age, when people live so much more slowly, they are somethings silver-

haired before fifty. And the other evidence is very strong.

2 v. *Eastward Ho*, ed. F. E. Shelling. Belles Lettres Series, Introduction.

1 v. *Eastward Ho*. Prologue.

2 *Westward Ho*, p. 237.

3 *Westward Ho*, pp. 217, 326.

4 *Westward Ho*, pp. 210, 235.

5 The end of 1603, of course. All the summer the plague was raging.

6 *a*. Dr Stoll (p. 63) finds in the Earl's discovery (*Westward Ho*, 233), of a hideous hag in the masked figure he had thought a beautiful woman, a possible reminiscene of Marton's *Sophonisba*, which may have been on the stage in 1603 or 1604. But the idea is a common enough one in all literatures. And if there is a debt, it might almost as easily be the other way. In any case, the date is not influenced.

b. If the autumn of 1604, then, of course, *Eastward Ho* must be put on to 1605.

1 Ed. Bullen: pp. 5, 6. The refernce is the more probable that *The Isle of Gulls* was written for the same company as *Eastward Ho*.

2 P. 16.

3 Stoll, p. 17.

4 Miss Hunt (*Thomas Dekker*, pp. 101-103) comes to much the same conclusion; *i.e. Westward Ho*, 1604, *Eastward Ho*,

1604-5, *Northward Ho*, 1605, as probable.

[1] Pp. 72-74.

[2] *The Collaboration of Webster and Dekker*, Chap. VI.

[3] Novella II., not I., as Dr Stoll gives it.

[4] v. *Celio Malespini und seine Novellen*: Misteli.

[1] See also a very sensible review of Mr Pierce's book by Dr P. Aronstein in *Beiblatt zur Anglia*, 1910, p. 79.

APPENDIX E.—"THE MALCONTENT"

The Malcontent was published in 1604, in two editions. The title-page of the first reads:

THE

MALCONTENT.

BY JOHN MARSTON.

The title-page of the second reads:

THE

MALCONTENT.

AUGMENTED BY MARSTON.

WITH THE ADDITIONS PLAYED BY THE KINGS MAJESTIES

SERVANTS.

WRITTEN BY JOHN WEBSTER.

The second edition differs from the first in having an Induction, and the insertion of twelve passages in the play.

Much fuss has been made about the amount of the play that Webster wrote. Dr Stoll[1] has conclusively shown that all we can deduce to be Webster's is the Induction; and Professor Vaughan has called attention to a final piece of evidence—that the Induction itself practically says that this is the case.

The matter is quite clear. The full-stop after "Servants" on the second title-page is what Dr Stoll calls "purely inscriptional." That the whole theory of Elizabethan punctuation rests on a psychological, not, as now, on a logical basis, has recently been shown with great force by Mr Simpson.[1] The whole look of the page makes it obvious that the intention was to connect Webster with the "Additions," and only with the additions, and to make Marston responsible for the augmentations as well as the bulk of the play. An æsthetic judgment of the play declares that the extra passages are all Marston's and that the Induction is probably not by Marston and probably is by Webster. And Burbadge, in the Induction, describing how the play fell into the hands of the King's Servants (from the Children of the Queen's Revels) and being asked "What are your additions?" makes answer, "Sooth, not greatly needful; only as your salad to your great feast, to entertain a little more time, and to abridge the not-received custom of music in our theatre." That probably, though not quite necessarily, identifies the "additions" with the Induction. There are three possible theories; that Marston wrote *The Malcontent* (first edition) and the extra passages, and Webster the Induction; that Marston wrote *The Malcontent* (first edition) and Webster the extra passages, and probably the Induction; or that originally Marston and Webster wrote the play together, and that for some reason only Marston's name appeared on the title-page. I think there is no reason to believe the third, every reason not to believe the second, and several reasons to believe the first. I do not think the arguments for *The Malcontent* dating from 1600, and for the "augmentations" being really restorations by Marston of cut pieces of his play in its first state, are decisive. But I think the case stands without these conclusions.[1]

Date.

As the first edition appeared without the Induction during 1604, and the second with it in the same year, and as it was obviously written for a special piratical revival by the King's Majesty's Servants, who claim the second edition, it is fair to suppose that the Induction was written during 1604.

[1] Pp. 55-60.

[1] *Shakespearian punctuation.* See also Professor Grierson's remarks on Elizabethan punctuation, *The Poems of John Donne*, vol. ii., pp. cxxi.-cxxiv.

[1] On the date of *The Malcontent* Dr Stoll goes off pursuing the wildest of goese through the undergrowth of a footnote. He "proves" a pharse to be in the "Ur-Hamlet" by taking it for granted that a play printed in 1604 is exactly as it was when it was written in 1600. The old assumption of the integrity of plays.

Appendix F.—"The White Devil."

Date.

The White Devil was printed in 1612. It obviously belongs to the same period as *The Duchess of Malfi.* That it is the earlier of the two is probable on general grounds, and proved by the advance of metrical license[1] and the absence of phrases and adaptations from the *Arcadia*, which are present in all Webster's later work.[2]

There are various clues, of more or less relevance, to its date:

Mr Percy Simpson has pointed out[3] that the puzzling and much emended passage about Perseus (p. 21; last line) is an allusion to Jonson's *Masque of Queens* (1609); a work Webster knew, for he borrows in *A Monumental Column* from the dedication to it.

> P. 23. MONTICELSO. Away with her!
> Take her hence!
> VITTORIA. A rape! a rape!
> MONTICELSO. HOW?
> VITTORIA. Yes, you have ravished Justice;
> Forced her to do your pleasure.

Dr Stoll suggests that Vittoria's cry, in its suddenness as

219

well as in the words, is very like Sebastian's in Tourneur's *The Atheist's Tragedy*, I. 4. But any connection between the two is doubtful; if there is any, Tourneur may have imitated Webster; and anyhow the date of *The Atheist's Tragedy* is still quite uncertain—1607-1611 is the most definite limit one can venture, and even that rather depends on accepting the anonymous *Revenger's Tragedy* as Tourneur's. This passage is more likely to be connected with *The Tragedy of Chabot*, V. 11, 122, "unto this he added a most prodigious and fearful rape, a rape even upon Justice itself. . . ." Professor Parrott thinks Chapman may have written this (it is in his part of the play) about 1612. And Webster admired and imitated Chapman. But the whole thing is too cloudy for the resemblance to be more than interesting.

The number of references to Ireland in the play is remarkable.[1] Either Webster had been in Ireland, or he had been hearing about it; or he had been reading a book on it. If it was a book, Barnaby Rich's *A New Description of Ireland*, 1610, has been suggested. It is very probable; for the book mentions the various subjects of Webster's references. But as there is no verbal connection, and as they are all things one could easily pick up by hearsay, the proof is not conclusive. No doubt, too, there were other books on Ireland at the time which might have contained such obvious journalistic prattle as this. Still, Rich's book is the best explanation of

Webster's mind being so full of Irish facts at the time: and the references are scattered enough to make a little against them having been introduced in a revision. For what this sort of evidence is worth, it points to 1610 or after.

Dr Stoll attaches importance to the preface and postscript. These, it would in any case be extremely probable, were written in 1612 for the publication of the book. And a pretty conclusive borrowing of phrase from Jonson's preface to *Cataline* (1611)[1] confirms this. Dr Stoll thinks the tone of the preface shows that the performance was recent. It is difficult to see why. Webster merely says that the play has been performed, without much success. His only hint about the time that has elapsed since lies in "and that, since that time [*i.e.* the time of the performance], I have noted most of the people that come to that playhouse resemble those ignorant asses, who, visiting stationers' shops, their use is not to inquire for good books but new books. . . ." This looks as if some time had gone by between the performance and the writing of the preface. He had had time to see and deplore *The White Devil* being forgotten by the "ignorant asses" who only wanted "new" goods. An interval of some months should be allowed at least.

The preface gives the further information that the performance had been in winter, and that the play had taken a long time in writing.

There is one more point. Dekker, writing an Epistle Dedicatory to *If This be not a Good Play*[1] addressed to the Queen's Servants (who produced *The White Devil*), wishes well to a new play by a "worthy friend" of his. It has been suggested that this means *The White Devil*. Dekker and Webster were old friends, and the vague complimentary epithets of the play apply.[2] It may be so. But as between twenty and thirty new plays were produced every year,[3] and the Queen's Servants, no doubt, contributed their share, there were a good many other plays Dekker might have been thinking of, and we cannot regard this as more than a possible conjecture. *If This be not a Good Play* was probably written and played in 1610 or 1611. The Epistle Dedicatory for the printed edition would probably be written for the occasion, *i.e.* in 1612 or the end of 1611. So any weight this conjecture has would point to Webster's play being produced in the beginning of 1612.[4]

The similarity of style and atmosphere and the close resemblance of a great many passages[1] (*not* verbal repetitions, far more subtle and convincing things than that) make it desirable to put *The White Devil* and *The Duchess of Malfi* as close together as possible. The tenuous evidence we have noticed points, if anywhere at all, to agreement with this— that is, to putting *The White Devil* on towards its final limit of 1612. Acknowledging that it is all quite uncertain, I think it is most probable that the play was written during 1611 and performed at the end of that year or in January or February 1612. It may have been written 1610 and performed 1610-1611. It would need some strong new evidence to put it back further.

Sources.

Some time and trouble have been spent in seeking an exact printed source for *The White Devil*, but, so far, in vain. The actual events, which took place in the end of the sixteenth century—Vittoria was born in 1557, was murdered in 1585—were well-known.[2] Did Webster get the story from an accurate history, from some romantic version, or from hearsay? One can only surmise. Professor Vaughan, who goes at greatest length into this question, thinks it quite possible the source was a novel or play, or an oral account, but is most in favour of Webster having read some fairly accurate contemporary account, and altered it for dramatic purposes. Webster's unusually accurate pronunciation of Italian names, and his quoting Tasso,[1] allow us to believe he may have known Italian. But the tale may well have got into an English or French version by 1610. The differences between Webster's version and the facts are queer. Many of them look certainly as if they had been made consciously (by Webster or someone else) for dramatic purposes; such as—besides the additions of madness and murders—the toning down of Lodovico to make him a minor figure, and the purification of Isabella. But there are others that have no such obvious point, the exchange of names between Marcello and Flamineo, the writing of Monticelso for Montalto,[2] and Paul IV. for Sixtus V. The first of these may be purposeful. Even one who has not read the Sixth Æneid may be able to perceive that Marcello is a pure young hero and Flamineo an amazing villain. Is it fanciful to more than suspect that *The White Devil* would be less effective if he were called Flamineo who died so innocently, and a Marcello played amazing tricks with bulletless pistols, or screamed in mock-death:

> "O I smell soot,
> Most stinking soot! The chimney is a-fire!
> My liver's parboil'd like Scotch holly-bread;
> There's a plumber laying pipes in my guts,
>   it scalds!"

It is not for nothing that you dare not call a hero Lord John or a villain George. And Webster, who had above all things a nose for irrelevant details that inexplicably trick you, unconscious, into the tone he desires, may have had a purpose in writing also Paulus for Sixtus, Monticelso for Montalto. Still, it is hard to think memory or report or notes did not play him false.

On the other hand such minute details from the

actual story have been preserved by Webster—names, the summer-house by the Tiber, and so on—that it is difficult to imagine that he got it from any scanty or oral report. And there are certain considerations which seem to favour his having worked from some extensive version, whether dramatic or in pamphlet form. Why should Brachiano and the Conjuror conduct their interview in Vittoria's house (p. 18)? No reason is given for the absurdity. There is an equally unexplained and apparently pointless incident in the trial-scene; where Brachiano refuses a chair, and sits on his cloak (pp. 19 and 22), to show, one gathers, his contempt for the Court. The labour and time Webster spent on the play, and his care in publishing this edition to wipe out the failure of the performance, forbid our explaining these things by hurry in composition, or by the text being printed from an acting version. They might well be the result of Webster's obvious lack of ordinary skill in dramatising a story of which he had a lengthy version before him. Such incidents as Francisco's sight of Isabella's ghost, and the spectacular and fairly accurate ceremony of choosing a Pope, as well as the divergencies in the characters of Francisco and Flamineo, as the play proceeds, also fit in well with this theory.

If Webster was working from some detailed account, it might either be a play or a narrative. In favour of the play are some of the extraordinary old-fashioned tags in *The White*

Devil, and particularly the amazing mixture of extremely fine and true lines and distressingly ludicrous couplets or phrases in the final scene (though such incongruities are far more possible for Webster than for any other great writer of the period). In this case, the characteristics of the dramatisation are due to the earlier play-wright.

On the other hand, the general line of the play gives the impression that Webster himself dramatised it directly.

In any case, from the details of names mentioned above, it looks as if someone, either Webster or an intermediate, had read some accurate account with care, making a few notes perhaps, had let it simmer into shape in his mind, the characters taking life and individuality, and then, later, written it out. Only so can the mistakes of memory be explained. Whether it was Webster who did this, or whether, as Professor Vaughan implies, he had someone else's account before him as he worked, it is impossible to say.

The State of the Play.

The White Devil is certainly entirely Webster's. It is also almost certain we have the whole play. There are no sure traces of revision for acting, or of abbreviation. Webster obviously, from his Preface, brought the play out with great self-consciousness and care, and a desire to see its merits recognised. So he would naturally print it complete. And both the Preface and general probabilities point to it having only been played once, not very successfully, before publication. So we need not suspect our copy of having been revised for a revival.

[1] *V.* Stoll, p. 190, metrical table.

[2] *V.* Crawford, *Collectanea* i., 20-46. It is very noticeable, and only to be explained by Webster having filled his notebook from the *Arcadia* after *The White Devil* and before *The Duchess of Malfi, A Monumental Column,* and *The Devil's Law-case.*

[3] *Modern Language Review*: January 1907.

[1] See p. 6. Irish gamesters: p. 16, no snakes in Ireland: p. 28, Irish rebels selling heads: p. 29 "like the wild Irish. . . ." : p. 31, Irish funerals.

[1] See Stoll, pp. 20, 21. Webster borrows most of this preface from prefaces of Jonson and Dekker.

[1] Printed 1612.

[2] "Such brave Triumphs of Poesy and elaborate industry . . ."

[3] *V.* Schelling, *Elizabethen Drama*, ii. pp. 371, 373. Malone and Fleay both suggest an average of twenty-three or four a year. This period was more prolific than the average, of course. For 1601-1611 Professor Schelling surmises a yearly average of nearer thirty.

[4] Dr Stoll offers the additional proof that Dekkar is speaking of a maiden effort, which *The White Devil* is. Mere

assumptions. Dekkar does not say the object of his interest is a maiden work. And nobody can state that *The White Devil* is.

¹ See for examples, Sampson, Introduction to *The White Devil*. etc., pp. xli-xliii. and Stoll, pp. 80-82.

² For detailed accounts see D. Gnoli, *Vittoria Accoramboni*. J. A. Symonds, in *italian By-ways* (1883): L. M'Cracken, *A Page of Forgotten History*.

¹ *The Duchess of Malfi*, p. 78.

² Dr Greg (*Modern Language Quarterly*: Dec. 1900) suggests that Webster may have misread (in, perhaps, a MSS. account) Moncelto for Montalto, and euphonised it into Monticelso, But the other difficulties remain.

Appendix G.—"The Duchess of Malfi."

Date.

The history of the various opinions about the date of *The Duchess of Malfi* is both entertaining and instructive. Dyce used to guess at 1616. Fleay put it back to 1612, a date which many slight indications favoured. These were mainly on stylistic and general grounds. Professor Vaughan, however, in 1900, made a suggestion which Dr Stoll, in 1905, worked out and regarded as providing conclusive evidence. So, according to the ordinary methods of dating plays, it did. It is not necessary to detail Dr Stoll's arguments. They refer to the oddly introduced passage in I, i. (p. 59) on the French King and his court. Dr Stoll rightly says it is very probable a passage like this in an Elizabethan play would refer to current events. He exhaustively proves that it does exactly fit what happened in France in the early part of 1617, when Louis XIII. had the evil counsellor Concini killed, "quitted" his palace of "infamous persons," and established a "most provident council"; events which made some stir in England at the time. As all this would have appeared in a different light in 1618 or after, and as there is other evidence that *The Duchess of Malfi* was being played in England at the end of

1617, we seem to have the date, the latter part of 1617, fixed with unusual certainty.[1] It is rare to be able to be so certain and so precise about an Elizabethan play. And having the date of composition of some thirty lines fixed, people would no doubt have gone on for ever believing they had the date of the whole fixed; had not Dr Wallace, delving in the Record Office, discovered that William Ostler, who played Antonio, died on December 16th, 1614![2] The explanation, of course, is that *The Duchess of Malfi* was written and performed before December 1614, and revived with additions in 1617. All the evidence we have shows that this habit of altering a play and putting in topical references whenever it was revived, was universal. Our modern reverence for the exact written word is the result of regarding plays as literary objects, and of our too careful antiquarian view of art. The Elizabethans would have thought it as absurd not to alter a play on revival as we think it to do so. They healthily knew that the life of a play was in its performance, and that the more you interested people by the performance, the better it was. The written words are one kind of raw material for a performance; not the very voice of God. So, naturally, they changed the play each time; and when we have the text of a play, all we can feel in the least certain about, is that we have it something as it was for the latest previous revival. Editors and critics have come to admit this, in general. But in individual instances they never remember to allow for it. Occasionally, as here, other circumstances are discovered, and put them right. But, on the whole, the common credulous assumption of certainty about dates in Elizabethan literature is as startling to an onlooker as the credulous assumption of certainty about authorship.

The Duchess of Malfi, then, was acted before December 1614; and as Webster obviously took as long over it as he confessedly did over *The White Devil*, the latest date we can give him for writing it is during the whole year of 1614. As it is later than *The White Devil*, we do not want to put it back beyond 1612, though as *The White Devil's* date is uncertain we could do so.

Strong internal evidence for the date of *The Duchess of Malfi* has, however, been pointed out by Mr Crawford.[1] His arguments rest mainly on the great similarity between *The Duchess of Malfi* and *A Monumental Column*. These are connected far more closely than any of Webster's works in several ways. The poem repeats both more words and lines and more ideas from *The Duchess of Malfi* than from any of the other plays. In metre it is, allowing for the different styles, nearer. If you examine the particular sources Webster borrowed from, the resemblance becomes even more obvious. In *The White Devil* he does not borrow from Sidney's *Arcadia* at all. In *The Devil's Law-Case* the borrowing is faint and patchy. In *The Duchess of Malfi* and *A Monumental Column* the borrowing is incessant and similar, and includes imitation of style. Another work both pieces borrow from, and only these two pieces among Webster's, is Donne's *An Anatomy of the World*, which was published in 1612.[1] There are also[2] in *The Duchess of Malfi* several imitations and borrowings of phrase from another book of 1612, Chapman's *Petrarch's Seven Penitential Psalms*. But the similarity itself of *A Monumental Column* and *The Duchess of Malfi* puts the date of the play further on than this. *A Monumental Column* is an elegy written in memory of Prince Henry, who died on November 6th, 1612. It was published in 1613, with similar elegies of Tourneur's and Heywood's. It appears to have been rather belated, for (lines 259-268) he refers to other elegies that had already appeared, and adds:

"For he's a reverend subject to be penn'd
Only by his sweet Homer and my friend."

i.e., only Chapman should write about the dead Prince. From this and from various reminiscences in *A Monumental Column*, Mr Crawford deduces that Webster must have seen Chapman's *Epicedium* on Prince Henry. I do not think it is proved; for the passage may only mean that Chapman ought to write an elegy. In any case, Chapman's poem followed the Prince's death so closely (as the other elegies Webster refers to also may well have done) that we cannot put *A Monumental*

Column much later for this. But (lines 102-5) there is a probable, though not certain, reference to Chapman's *The Masque of The Middle Temple* performed February 15, 1613. *A Monumental Column*, therefore, may be dated any time in the half-year December 1612-May 1613, with a slight preference for February and March 1613. As *The Duchess of Malfi* was certainly before the end of 1614, and certainly after the beginning of 1612, and as there is so much evidence that the play and the poem were being written at the same time, we may date the play with fair certainty at 1613, including perhaps the latter part of 1612.

There is no other evidence of any value for the date of *The Duchess of Malfi*. It may appear that I have been trying to establish the earlier limit by that method I have always decried elsewhere, namely, by dating the whole by the date of various passages. The answer is that in the case of *The Duchess of Malfi* and *A Monumental Column* the borrowings from other authors are so numerous, so widespread, and so much part of the whole play, that the likelihood of them having all been introduced in revision is very small. Such a revision would have to be a complete rewriting of the play. And while we must allow for the possibility of revision in any Elizabethan play, we cannot suppose that the writers of that age took the trouble to rewrite their plays, in tone, from beginning to end.

Sources.

It is certain that Webster got the story of *The Duchess of Malfi* from Painter's *Palace of Pleasure*, Novel XXIII. Painter had it from Belleforest, who had it from Bandello. A recent Italian book shews that Bandello probably based his account on the testimony of actors in the actual events, and suggests that he may even have been himself one of them, the one whom we know as Delio.[1] It is an alluring speculation.

Beyond this, the tortures of the Duchess were suggested, probably, by incidents in Sidney's *Arcadia*. The same book, which gave Webster so much even in phrases and sentences, may have been responsible for much in the Duchess's character, and for the echo-scene (V. 3). These are less certain. Mr Crawford with greater probability thinks that V. 1., the scene of Delio's and Julia's suits to Pescara, was suggested from Montaigne, Book I.[2]

State of the Play.

I have already explained some of the reasons for thinking there was a revival of *The Duchess of Malfi* in the latter half of 1617. They are, briefly, these. The first fifty lines of the play obviously refer to events which happened in France in April 1617, and roused immediate interest in England. They could not have been written after about May 1618, when these events were seen in a quite different light. Also, the chaplain to the Venetian Ambassador in England has left a description of a play he saw in London, which is probably, but not certainly, *The Duchess of Malfi*.[1] He did not get to London before the beginning of October 1617, and he seems to have seen the play a little time before the 7th February 1618.

The Actors list in the first edition allows of a revival of this date.

The Duchess of Malfi, then, was revived in a revised form in the latter part of 1617. That the beginning of the play was revised we know. If the Italian chaplain's account of the play be accurate, there must have been a good deal in the performance he saw which is not in the play as we have it— even allowing for his misinterpretation.

One passage in the play itself may point to a combination of two versions. In I. 1., Delio usefully questions Antonio about the other chief characters. Antonio gives a long description of the Cardinal; then a long description of the Duke, his brother; then, before going on to the Duchess, he reverts suddenly to the Cardinal, as if he had not mentioned him, with:

"Last, for his brother there, the Cardinal. . . ."

On the other hand, the inclusion in the first quarto (1623) of Middleton, Rowley, and Ford's commendatory verses, and of Webster's dedicatory letter, as well as, and more forcibly than, the avowal of the title-page,[1] go to show that this edition of the play is as Webster would have had it. It must, therefore, be fairly near the original version (1613); containing most of that, with whatever of subsequent additions or changes Webster supposed improvements. And we cannot doubt that practically all of the play, as we have it, is by Webster.

[1] See, for instance, Professor Schelling, *Elizabethan Drama, vol. i.* p. 590. "This fixes the date of *The Duchess of Malfi* at a time later than April, 1617, and puts to rest once and for all former surmises on the subject." This eternal rest lasted nearly five years.

[2] See *The Times*, Oct. 2 and 4, 1909.

[1] *Collectanea*, Series i. pp. 20-46, and especially Series ii. pp. 1-63.

[1] In its entirety. Without *The Second Anniversary* in 1611. But Webster borrows from the whole.

[2] Crawford *Collectanea*, ii. 55-58.

[1] *Giovanna d'Aragona, Duchessa d'Amalfi, da Domenico Morellini*, 1906. *V.* review by W. W. Greg in *Modern Language Review*, July 1907.

[2] *Collectanea*, ii. pp. 14, 15.

[1] *V.* Stoll, p. 29.

[1] "The perfect and exact Copy, with divers things printed, that the length of the play would not bear in presentment."

APPENDIX H.—"A MONUMENTAL COLUMN."

Date.

The question of the date of *A Monumental Column* is discussed in Appendix G. in connection with *The Duchess of Malfi.* It must have been written within some six months after November 1612; probably about March 1613.

Sources.

There is, of course, no special source for a poem like this. It repeats the usual thoughts in elegies of its kind; and borrows largely in expressions and in general style from Donne; also from Sidney, Chapman, and Ben Jonson.

APPENDIX I.—"THE DEVIL'S LAW-CASE"

Date.

The Devil's Law-Case was published in 1628. There is little evidence to decide the date of its writing.

(1) There is a reference (IV. 2) to an affray in the East Indies:

"How! go to the East Indies! and so many Hollanders gone to fetch sauce for their pickled herrings! Some have been peppered there too lately"

This almost certainly refers to a Dutch attack in August 1619 on some English ships engaged in loading pepper. News seems to have taken from nine to fifteen months to travel between England and the East Indies. London might learn, then, of this pepper business any time in the latter half of 1620. The word "lately," and still more the comparative unimportance and transience of the event, suggest that the form of the play in which this sentence occurred was being acted towards the end of 1620 or in the first half of 1621. If that form was the only form, we cannot tell; and we have no right to assume it. The whole of the reference to the East Indies is comprised in a few sentences in this one place. It is entirely unnecessary to the pilot, and it could easily have been inserted at a moment's notice.

(2) It is said that the chief idea in the play, Leonora's attempt to bastardise her son by confessing a long-past adultery that as a matter of fact never took place, resembles stories in the pseudo-Marlovian *Lust's Dominion, The Spanish Curate*, by Fletcher and Massinger, and *The Fair Maid of the Inn*, by Massinger and another. *The Fair Maid of the Inn* was probably not written before 1624. *The Spanish Curate* was written between March and October 1622. It is only just possible that *The Devil's Law-Case* can have been written after it.[1] *Gerardo the Unfortunate Spaniard*, an English translation from the Spanish, which appeared in March 1622 and was the source of *The Spanish Curate*, may also have suggested this part of *The Devil's Law-Case*. But resemblances are tricky things. This one, closely examined, turns out to depend largely on having the confession of a past misdemeanour at a public trial. And to bring in a public trial is exactly the thing that would independently occur to the mind of a dramatist of *circa* 1620, if he imagined or heard of the rest of the story. The only resemblance that really may mean anything is to *Lust's Dominion*, where a widow has a grudge against her son, because of a man she is in love with. So, to defame him and deprive him of the inheritance, she invents, with details, and publicly confesses, a story which makes him a bastard. The motives and feelings

of the characters in this play correspond far more than in those others, to *The Devil's Law-Case* situation. It is true *Lust's Dominion* is an old play of 1590. But it may have been revived and revised many times. Perhaps it "suggested" the idea of *The Devil's Law-Case*—in any of the million ways, direct and indirect, in which, in real life, ideas are suggested. But the truth is that, unless a very certain source is known, the search for the suggestion of so unexotic an idea as this becomes rather foolish. A half-remembered story, a friend's anecdote, an inspiration—anything may be responsible for any proportion of it. It may be useful to trace John Keats' hippocrene; not his porridge.

(3)[1] The title-page says that the play was "approvedly well acted by Her Majesty's Servants." This company, which also performed *The White Devil*, was called by this name until March 1619, when Queen Anne died. It appears to have gone gradually to pieces after that. Thomas Heywood, for instance, seems to have left it by 1622. In July 1622 it was reconstructed, with children as well as adults, as "The Players of the Revels." It probably broke up in the next year. The point is, under what name did it go between 1619 and 1622? Under the old one of "Her Majesty's Servants," thinks Dr Stoll. Mr Murray, the latest investigator of the history of the Dramatic Companies, says it was called by the name of "The Red Bull," its theatre. What evidence there is seems to indicate this. The corresponding (or same) company on tour was generally known as "The late Queen Anne's players." We should have expected one of these two latter names, if the play had been performed only between 1619 and 1622. This consideration by itself makes a slight, a quite slight, probability of the play being acted before March 1619.

Altogether, therefore, we can only say that the play is earlier than July 1622, and was almost certainly being acted in some form in about August 1620-July 1621. Everything else is quite uncertain; except that the nature of the play forbids you to look earlier than, at earliest, 1610. The tiny probability of 1620 or after, for the whole play, established by the East Indies reference, is about balanced by the tiny probability of before 1619, established by the name of the Company. For charts and lists one would say 1620.

Sources.

Perhaps, for the main idea. *Lust's Dominion.* See under *Date* (2). The episode of Romelio's remedial stabbing is from Goulart's *Histoires Admirables*, probably in Grimeston's translation (1607); a source Webster used also for his lycanthropy in *The Duchess of Malfi.*

The State of the Play.

There is no reason to suppose that any part of the play is not by Webster, or that it has been much abbreviated or revised. The title-page (1623) avows it "the true and perfect copy, from the original." It may be true. But that the original may have borne signs of alterations for stage purposes, is suggested by the fact that (pp. 126, 127) on three separate occasions in III. 3, the 1623 edition has "Surgeon" where it ought to be "Surgeons," for there were two surgeons in the case. It would have lessened the dramatic effect but not hurt the plot to reduce these two to one, and it is just the kind of change that might have been made in order to use fewer actors. Her Majesty's Servants were on the downhill when they acted this play. And if this change was made for acting, others may have been.

¹ *V.* Stoll, p. 32.

¹ For this paragraph *v. English Dramatic Companies* 1558-1642, by John Tuoker Murray: esp. vol. i. pp. 193-200.

APPENDIX J.—"A CURE FOR A CUCKOLD"

Date.

A Cure for a Cuckold was published in 1661.

(1) It is necessary at one point that a sea-fight should have taken place and be narrated. The English merchant-ships are reported to have been attacked by three Spanish men-of-war, off Margate. From its style this play must date from the end of James', or from Charles', reign. At any period the dramatist would be likely to attribute fighting, in a play of contemporary life, to the actual enemies of England of the time; and at this period he would be especially unlikely to offend by suggesting enmity with any friend of the rulers of the country. So we may find it probable these lines were written between 1624 and 1630 (inclusive), when England and Spain were at war; not earlier, while Charles' fantastic matrimonial expedition was going on, and not later, when peace had been patched up. The fact that England was more importantly at war with France from 1627, tends a little to narrow it to 1624-1627. This is a moderate proof of the date of these lines, or one of them; a proportionately smaller one, therefore, for the whole play.

(2) The plot of "Webster's portion" of *A Cure for a*

Cuckold is the same as, or similar to, that of other plays. It is a particular form of the favourite Elizabethan *motif*, Mistress—Lover—Friend. On this point I have little to add to and not much to subtract from Dr Stoll's arguments. The bulk of mine are a summation of his. He seems to me to prove his point; not as conclusively as he believes; still, to prove it.

In giving a synopsis of the relevant parts of the plots of these plays I shall, for clearness' sake, call the protagonist— the lover—A, the friend F, and the Lady L.

(*a*) In Marston's *Dutch Courtezan* (1604) L (a courtezan) and F are in love first. F chucks her. L, for revenge, encourages A, who has conceived an overwhelming passion for her; and promises herself to him if he will kill F. A promises to do so; on reflection repents, and warns F. They agree on a trick together, feign a quarrel, and pretend to fight a duel. F hides, and is given out as slain in the duel. To punish A for his folly he hides also from him. L, to complete her vengeance, has A arrested for murder. As A finds he cannot produce F to clear himself, he is in a bad way. At the last moment F, present in disguise, reveals himself. L is led off to prison. A is cured of his passion; and all is for the best.

(*b*) In Massinger's *The Parliament of Love* (1624) A and L have been contracted in marriage; A has, impatiently, first proposed, and then forcibly attempted copulation before the marriage-ceremony; and L is consequently possessed by hatred for him. The tale is told in four scenes. (II. 2) A insists on seeing L and offers to do anything she likes to obtain her pardon, and her. She accepts the bargain, and bids him find out his best friend and kill him.

(III. 2) A soliloquises that he has tried many friends with a proposal and none of them has turned out a true one. Enter F, who is ecstatic over an unhoped meeting with *his* mistress, which she has appointed for two hours hence. A is melancholy and tries to slip away. F insists on knowing the reason. A says he has to fight a duel shortly, and can't find a second. F insists on coming as second, and cutting his mistress, in spite of A's protestations.

(IV. 2) They arrive at the duel-ground. A makes F swear to fight relentlessly; then reveals the truth, he himself (A) is the ever detestable enemy. He insists on fighting, is beaten, but not killed.

(V. 1) It is common talk that A has killed F, and that L has had A arrested for trial before "The Parliament of Love."

At the trial A is found guilty of murder, L of cruelty, and condemned. L repents and forgives A. F, supposed (by a trick arranged, presumably, with A) to be dead, rises from his bier. All is put right, and A and L marry.

(*c*) In *A Cure for a Cuckold*, L (Clare) is secretly in love with F (Bonvile), who has been married, on the morning the play begins, to somebody else. The tale is told in five scenes.

(I. 1) L is sad. A (Lessingham) renews a previous proposal to her. L will accept on one condition. A agrees. L tells him it is to find out and kill his best friend.

(I. 2) A soliloquises. Enter some friends, and demand the reason of A's sadness. A says he must fight a duel next morning at Calais, and has no second; seconds to fight. He asks each to be his second. They refuse and exeunt. Enter F; demands to know the reason of A's sadness. A reluctantly explains. F offers to come, and cut his wedding-night. A protests. F insists, in spite of the arrival on the scene of his newly-married wife.

(III. 1) They arrive at the duel-ground. A says he has come to fight an innocent enemy; *i.e.* F, he reveals. And he is so deep in love, he says, he must kill him. F quibbles that as a "friend" he now *is* dead. They part.

(IV. 2) A reports to L F's death. L confesses her unhappy love for F and declares herself over-joyed. A turns against her.

After some complications with the other part of the plot, (V. 2) A and L are reconciled, and marry.

Before we can proceed to the comparison of these plots there is one point in *A Cure for a Cuckold* to be got clear. That is, Clare's motive in giving Lessingham the command. There are various remarks about it in the play. In I. 2, Lessingham, in his soliloquy, rather meekly wonders "what might her hidden purpose be in this?" He can only suggest that she has a psychological interest in proving the proposition that there is no such thing as friendship. In II. 4, Bonvile's absence is commented on. Clare, in an aside, says:

I fear myself most guilty for the absence
Of the bridegroom. What our wills will do
With over-rash and headlong peevishness
To bring our calm discretions to repentance!
Lessingham's mistaken, quite out o' the way
Of my purpose, too.

In III. 1, in the dialogue between the friends, Lessingham has a new reason to suggest:

. . . She loathes me, and has put,
As she imagines, this impossible task,
For ever to be quit and free from me.

In III. 3. When the news comes that Bonvile is at Calais, as Lessingham's "second," Clare guesses the truth, and cries, *aside again*:

O fool Lessingham
Thou hast mistook my injunction utterly
Utterly mistook it! . . .
I fear we both are lost.

In IV. 2. Lessingham reports to Clare that he has fulfilled

her injunctions.

    CLARE. Then of all men you are most miserable:
      Nor have you ought furthered your suit in this,
      Though I enjoined you to 't; for I had thought
      That I had been the best esteemed friend
      You had i' the world.
    LESS. Ye did not wish, I hope,
    That I should have murdered you.
    CLARE. You shall perceive more
      Of that hereafter. . . .
She asks who the slain friend is, and hears
"Bonvile." At first she is "lost for ever." Then she
suddenly changes and professes great pleasure,
promises instantly to marry Lessingham, because
he has rid her of her "dearest friend and fatalest
enemy"—she was in love with Bonvile:

    And beholding him
    Before my face wedded unto another,
    And all my interest in him forfeited,
    I fell into despair; and at that instant
    You urging your suit to me, and I thinking
    That I had been your only friend i' the world,
    I heartily did wish you would have killed
    That friend yourself, to have ended all my sorrow,
    And had prepared it, that unwittingly

You should have done 't by poison.

Later, Lessingham turns against her, and leaves her.

She, in a soliloquy, expresses great remorse:

I am every way lost, and no means to raise me

But blessed repentance . . .

. . . Now I suffer.

Deservedly.

Bonvile appears. She rejoices to find him alive. After some conversation—

CLARE (giving Bonvile a letter)

. . . had you known this which I meant to have sent you,

An hour 'fore you were married to your wife,

The riddle had been construed.

BON. Strange! This expresses

    That you did love me.

CLARE. With a violent affection.

BON. Violent indeed; for it seems it was your purpose

To have ended it in violence on your friend:

The unfortunate Lessingham unwittingly

Should have been the executioner.

CLARE. 'Tis true.

In V. 2 she again expresses contrition to Lessingham:

> CLARE.   It was my cause
> That you were so possessed; and all these troubles
> Have from my peevish will original;
> I do repent, though you forgive me not.

Dr Stoll's impression is that Clare's motive is mainly meant to be jealousy of Bonvile (F) and a desire for his death, but that occasionally obscurity comes in and that she seems to have meant something else. As the motive in *The Dutch Courtezan* was also jealous hatred of F, while that in *The Parliament of Love* was hatred of A, this tells a little against Dr Stoll's idea that *The Parliament of Love* came between *The Dutch Courtezan* and *A Cure for a Cuckold*. He brings the "obscurity of motivation" into service, however, by an ingenious theory of Webster starting with a plot where the motive was jealousy of F, and introducing phrases and ideas (*e.g.* "Kill for my sake the friend that loves thee dearest") from the other, *Parliament of Love*, motivation of offended modesty.

But this will not do. It is impossible to imagine that Webster had a mind with so extraordinarily feeble a grasp. And an inspection of the relevant passages, quoted above, shows the truth. Lessingham's own conjectures, of course, are astray. He is meant not to know what Clare is at. The only place which favours the view that her motive was a jealous desire for Bonvile's death is where she confesses it to him, near the end of the play. If this is true, it is absolutely at variance with the rest of the play, which is perfectly concordant with itself. We do not know, at the beginning of the play, that Lessingham's best friend is Bonvile. Nor, as far as we can see, does she. She once says, and once practically admits, to Lessingham, that her command really meant that he was to kill *her*. And—which far outweighs anything said to another person, for that might be a lie—she twice, *in an aside*, says that Lessingham mistook her words and is doing something she did not intend. It is perfectly plain and indisputable. She was not aiming at Bonvile. Her remorse for her folly was natural, and does not demand the jealousy-of-Bonvile theory. And her statement to Bonvile must be explained away.

It might be suggested that it was a desperate lie, and that the whole thing is a bad attempt at subtle psychology. Or much more probably, that it is an instance of the dangers that lurk for collaboration, especially if it is not contemporaneous; and that one of the two authors, probably Rowley, misunderstood a part of the plot the other was responsible for, and innocently roused confusion. But I think the severer course of emendation can be shown to be absolutely necessary.

For if you look at the passage (the last one quoted from IV. 2) you will see it is really *impossible* that "your friend" can refer to Bonvile, as it seems to. It makes nonsense of the whole passage! For in that case all the information he gets from the letter is that she loves him. And how would that have construed "the riddle?" For the "riddle" included, by this hypothesis, her queer injunction to Lessingham and its hidden intention to end in Bonvile's death; all of which Bonvile would be ignorant of, an hour before his marriage, and which she'd be scarcely likely to reveal to him! Moreover, what does "unwittingly" mean! How do you kill a man "unwittingly," if you challenge him to a duel in order to kill him? The whole thing is mad.

Of course, some small change has to be made in the text. Either "on your friend" must be changed to "on yourself"; or, more probably, "and" should be read for "on," and the whole should be punctuated:

"To have ended it with violence; and your friend, The unfortunate Lessingham, unwittingly," etc.

and the whole tale is this. She gives him a letter which he was to have opened just before his marriage. He reads it. It tells him, first, that she loved him. He goes on reading, "Violent, indeed; . . . for it seems . . ." It seems, from the letter, that she had intended to "end" (the word fits, by this interpretation) her violent love with violence on herself. She was going to have had poison given her. And Lessingham was going to have done it, "unwittingly." She has told

252

Lessingham the whole story five minutes before (p. 309) in the same scene (*v.* the preceding quotation but one). She even used the same word, "unwittingly." Bonvile was to have learnt of her love and of her death at the same moment, and "the riddle had been construed."

I have spent some time over this point in order to show that Webster (or Webster and Rowley) is perfectly clear in his motivation in *A Cure for a Cuckold*, and that the motive was this. For it removes the only argument in favour of *A Cure for a Cuckold* preceding *The Parliament of Love*; and it may counteract the impression that might be produced by Dr Stoll's harping on Webster's inability to make a plot with coherence or even normal sanity.

To go back to the comparison of Massinger's, Marston's, and Webster's plays; when they are summarised in that way, it becomes immediately obvious either that there is some special connection between *The Parliament of Love* and *A Cure for a Cuckold*, or that they have a common source other than *The Dutch Courtezan*. There are so many similarities; the whole dramatisation of the tale and division into scenes, the "dearest friend" command, the search for him under pretext of asking for a second in a duel, the unsuccessful application to other friends, F cutting his mistress, the duel scene, the supposed death of F, and so on. They cannot possibly have arisen from independent study of Marston's play.

There may have been an intermediate step, a source, perhaps, in the first twenty years of the seventeenth century, and, if so, probably founded on Marston's play. Dr Stoll does not consider the possibility of this. But we cannot rule it out. It would explain the general similarity, with such differences of motivation, etc., in Webster's and Massinger's plays. This intermediate source must have been either itself a play or a story that fell very easily and necessarily into certain scenes, as an apparently whole, already carved, chicken drops, as soon as you touch it, into neatly severed limbs. More than this one cannot say. There is little proof for or against an intermediate source. One can only admit its possibility.

But if only these three plays are left us, which was intermediate, *The Parliament of Love* or *A Cure for a Cuckold*? The former is nearer to *The Dutch Courtezan* in one point, the law-case at the end, in which L accuses A; the latter in no point. This is some evidence, but not so strong as it seems, for the law-case at the end of *The Parliament of Love* is required anyhow by the whole plot, independently of this part. Then there are certain differences in treatment that may be significant. Webster comments on the strangeness of the seconds having to fight in the duel. Massinger accepts it without comment. Dr Stoll thinks this a proof that Webster was the later. To me it seems more likely that the inventor of the story should have commented on a detail like this, and the man who took the story over, accepted it. Again, Webster directly presents A trying several friends in vain before he tries F; Massinger only relates it. Is it more likely that Webster dramatised what Massinger reported, or that Massinger made indirect what Webster gave directly? The former, I think; so that this piece of evidence favours Massinger being the intermediary. Dr Stoll suggests several pieces of more general evidence. (1) *A Cure for a Cuckold* shows the influence of Fletcher and Massinger. This would have happened if Webster had been imitating *The Parliament of Love*. Therefore he was imitating it. (2) Webster could not have invented so dramatic a sequence of scenes himself; and Massinger—and only Massinger—could. (8) Webster's muddling of motivation shows that he was trying to work *The Parliament of Love* motives into a different plot. (4) The mass of word-play and quibbling in Webster shows he was later, an embroiderer. (5) Some of the later invented incidents, *e.g.*, the duel-scene, and also the struggle in A's soul, are Massingerish.

These are not really at all strong. (1) is bad logic. Webster would have shown—and did show—the influence of the time anyhow. (2) These generalisations about Webster's capabilities, founded on such small data, are very dangerous. Possibly Webster could have invented these scenes. Certainly Rowley, his collaborator, could. Massinger was not the only person. (8) I have disposed of. (4) has some weight: but as Webster was fond of these queer notions and verbal tricks (he still kept something of his heritage from Donne), and Massinger was less fond, it is not very convincing. (5) also has a little weight, but it is again dangerous to suppose that Webster and Rowley, writing in the manner of Massinger's period, could not have caught something of that very second-rate magic. In any case the struggle in A's soul comes in *The Dutch Courtezan*, and *ex hypothesi* Webster could have used it, even if he hadn't the brains to think of it.

Parts of some of these arguments, it may also be worth remarking, especially of (2) and (5), depend on *The Dutch Courtezan*, or something equally remote, being the immediate source of whichever of *The Parliament of Love* and *A Cure for a Cuckold* was the earlier.

So far there has been a little evidence of the priority of Massinger's play. Dr Stoll advances one more proof. He shows the evolution of various fragments of the *Dutch Courtezan—Parliament of Love* story, through forms that must have been familiar to Massinger. To begin with, there is *The Scornful Lady* (1609, or 10) by Beaumont and Fletcher. Massinger, who was a close student of their work, must have known it. In this play the elder Loveless has forced a kiss in public from the Lady. She condemns him to face the Channel, a year in France, and a French mistress. He goes and soon returns in disguise, to report his own death; which scares her, for a minute, into confessing that she did love him. There is really very little of relevance in this: far less than Dr Stoll makes out.[1] But it has a certain resemblance to *The Parliament of Love*.

The next instance is more interesting. *The Little French Lawyer* (1619 or 20), by Fletcher and Massinger, has a variant of the story. In this, A and F are going, as principal and second, to fight a duel. L gives A a sudden command, which will cause him to cut the duel and sacrifice his friend. There is the struggle between love and friendship, in A's breast. Love wins. This is a curious modification of the other theme; but the similarity is not really great. There are minor details of resemblance, which Dr Stoll brings out clearly,[1] though he exaggerates the main points. Most, at least, of this story in *The Little French Lawyer*, comes in Massinger's portion of the play.[2]

These two steps do not amount to much, but they help a little. We can see that Massinger's mind was familiar with variants of the story and similar situations. Since a comparison of his variant and Webster's has also made it seem more likely that Webster imitated him, we may conclude that if *The Dutch Courtezan*, *The Parliament of Love*, and *A Cure for a Cuckold* are the only plays in the matter, that was probably the order in which they were written. *The Parliament of*

Love was licensed in November 1624, so 1625—is, by this department of the evidence, a probable date.

We can only say then that this play was very likely written between 1625 and 1642; and rather more probably before 1630 than after.

QUESTIONS OF AUTHORSHIP

A Cure for a Cuckold was first printed in 1661 by Kirkman, as by Webster and Rowley. This evidence is of very little value. That Webster's hand is to be found faintly in several parts of the play is shown with probability, but not certainty, by Dr Stoll.[1] His parallel passages seem to be the only proofs of his that have any validity. Beyond this we can say nothing; except that the under-plot, the Compass affair, is probably not by Webster, and certainly might be by Rowley. How much share Rowley or anybody else had in the other part of the play, cannot be settled, at least without much more minute investigation than this problem has yet received. Mr Spring-Rice's and Mr Gosse's subtraction of the main plot of the play, and publication of it by itself (as by Webster), satisfies one's artistic feeling, more than one's desire for correct attribution.

[1] Dr Stoll's great fault is that he is given to pressing evidence, carelessly and unfairly, in his own direction. He is too eager to prove a case. In this instance a notable one, he says, that the elder Loveless "elicits" from the Lady, "a

rueful declaration, like Leonora's in the *Parliament of Love*, that were he alive she would marry him." It is a concoction of untruths. All the Lady says is that if she *had* been warned when Loveless was setting out, "these two arms had been his sea." As for Leonora she says nothing of the kind. All she says is that, rather than that Cleremond be executed and she live and die an anchoress in an eight-foot room built on his grave, she'll marry him. Cleremond is not dead, and nobody thinks he is. Perhaps Dr Stoll was thinking of Bellisant, who is driven by the supposed death of Montrose to confess she loved him. But that belongs to another part of the plot.

[1] Stoll, 168-170.

[2] *i.e.*, in Act I.(C.H.E.L. VI, pp. 139, 9).

[1] Pp. 37-41.

APPENDIX A.—"APPIUS AND VIRGINIA."

[THE original form of this appendix was rearranged and shortened by the author for separate publication in the *Modern Languages Review*, vol. viii. No. 4 (October 1913). I have here combined the two versions, following the order of the second, but restoring most of the passages which were omitted from it to save space.

E. M.]

BIBLIOGRAPHY

A. EDITIONS

B. CRITICISM, SOURCES, ETC.

A. EDITIONS

The Works of John Webster. Collected by the Rev. Alexander Dyce. Four volumes, 1830. Reprinted 1857, one volume.

The Dramatic Works of John Webster. Edited by William Hazlitt. Four volumes. Library of Old Authors. 1857.

The White Devil and Duchess of Malfy. Ed. Sampson. 1904. Belles Lettres Series.

The Mermaid Series: Webster and Tourneur. Edited by J. A. Symonds, with introduction. 1888. Contains *The White Devil* and *The Duchess of Malfi.*

The White Devil; or, The Tragedy of Paulo Giordano Ursini, Duke of Brachiano, with The Life and Death of Vittoria Corombona, the famous Venetian Curtizan. Acted by the Qwenes Majesties Servants. 1612, quarto. Reprinted 1631, quarto. Reprinted 1665, quarto. Reprinted 1672, quarto.

Injur'd Love; or, The Cruel Husband. By N[ahum] Tate. A Version of *The White Devil.* 1707.

The White Devil. A Select Collection of Old Plays, vol.

iii., Dodsley. 1744. Reprinted 1780. Notes by Isaac Reed. Dodsley.

The White Devil. The Ancient British Drama, vol. iii. Edited by Sir Walter Scott. 1810.

The White Devil. A Select Collection of Old Plays, Notes by Reed, Gilchrist, and the Editor (Collier 1825).

Vittoria Corrombona, ou le Diable Blanc. Contemporains de Shakespeare. J. Webster et J. Ford. Traduits par Ernest Lafond. Paris, 1865.

Vittoria Corombona. Alt-englisches Theater. Herausgegeben von Robert Prolss. Two volumes. Leipzig.

The Tragedy of the Dutchesse of Malfy. Quarto, 1623. Reprinted 1640, quarto. Reprinted 1678, quarto.

The Duchesse of Malfy. 1660 (*circa*), quarto. Probably reprint of first Quarto (*v.* Sampson, *Webster's White Devil,* etc., p. 404).

The Unfortunate Dutchesse of Malfy; or The Unnatural Brothers. Written by Mr Webster. 1708, quarto (printed from 1678 edition for stage purposes).

The Fatal Secret. A Tragedy. As acted at the Theatre Royal. By Lewis Theobald. A version of *The Duchess of Malfi,* 1735. (Preface avows Webster's authorship.)

The Duchesse of Malfy. The Ancient British Drama. 1810. (Printed from 1670 Ed.)

The Duchess of Malfi. Tallis's Acting Drama, part i., 1851.

(Altered and expurgated.)

Die Herzogin von Amalfi. Shakespeare's Zeitgenossen und ihre Werke, 1858-1860. F. von Bodenstedt. ("The Duchess" is translated, the other plays summarised.)

La Duchesse d' Amalfi. 1865. (Translated by Lafond.)

The Duchess of Malfi. The Works of the British Dramatists. John Keltie. 1870.

The Duchess of Malfi. Dick's standard Plays. 1883.

The Duchess of Malfi. The Best Elizabethan Plays. Edited by W. R. Thayer. 1892. (Expurgated.)

The Duchess of Malfi. Temple Dramatists. Edited C. Vaughan. 1896.

The Duchess of Malfi. Ed. W. A. Neilson.

The Malcontent. By John Marston. 1604.

The Malcontent. Augmented by Marston. With the additions played by the King's Majesty's Servants. Written by John Webster. 1604.

The Famous History of Sir Thomas Wyat. With the Coronation of Queen Mary and the Coming in of King Philip. As it was plaid by the Queens Majesties' Servants. Written by Thomas Dickers and John Webster. 1607. Reprinted in Two Old Plays. Ed. W. J. Blew. 1876.

North-Ward Ho. By Thomas Decker and John Webster. 1607.

West-Ward Ho. Sundry Times acted by the Children of

Paules. Written by Tho. Dekker and John Webster. 1607.

The Devil's Law-Case; or, When Women goe to Law, the Devil is full of businesse. A new Trage-comedy by John Webster. 1623.

Appius and Virginia. A Tragedy by John Webster. 1654.

A Cure for a Cuckold. A Pleasant Comedy. Written by John Webster and William Rowley 1661.

The Thracian Wonder. A Comical History by John Webster and William Rowley. 1661.

Love's Graduate. A Comedy by John Webster. 1885. Edited by Stephen Spring-Rice. With an introduction by Edmund Gosse. [Merely *A Cure for a Cuckold* with the sub-plot, the Compass story left out.]

Monuments of Honor. Derived from remarkable antiquity and celebrated . . . at the sole munificent charge . . . of the Worshipfull Fraternity of the Eminent Merchant Taylors. Invented and written by John Webster, Merchant Taylor. 1624.

A Monumental Columne erected to the living Memory of the ever-glorious Henry, late Prince of Wales. By John Webster. 1613.

B. CRITICISM, SOURCES, ECT.

Retrospective Review. 1823. *John Webster* [anonymous article].

A True Relation of the deserved Death of that base and

Insolent Tyrant, the most unworthy Marshall of France. . . . A True Recital of those things that have been done in the Court of France since the Death of Marshall D'Ancre. 1617.

J. Q. Adams, Junior. Greene's *Menaphon* and *The Thracian Wonder*. Modern Philology, iii. 1906.

W. Archer. *Webster, Lamb, and Swinburne*. New Review, 1893. [Decrying Webster and the "Lamb Tradition" about the Elizabethans.]

M. Bandello. *Novelle*. 1554-73

F. de Boaistuau and P. Belleforest. *Histoires Tragiques*. 1580-2.

J. le G. Brereton, 1909. *Elizabethan Drama*. [Contains revised version of the review of Prof. Sampson's *The White Devil* and *The Duchess of Malfi*, which appeared in *Hermes*, November 1905.]

J. le Gay Brereton. *The Relation of the Thracian Wonder to Greene's Menaphon*. Mod. Language Review, October 1906. Englische Studien. xxxvii., 1907.

Crawford, C. *Collectanea*. Two Series. 1906-7. Series I., pp. 20-46. Webster and Sidney. Series II., pp. 1-63. Webster, Maraton, Montaigne, Donne, etc. Reprinted from *Notes and Queries*.

Gnoli, D. *Vittoria Accoramboni*. 1870.

Gosse, Edmund. *Seventeenth Century Studies*, 1883. John Webster.

Greg, W. W. *Webster's White Devil*. Modern Language Quarterly, Dec. 1900.

Grimeston. Translation of Goulart's *Histoires admirables et mémorables de nostre temps*. 1607.

Hatcher, O. L. *Sources and Authorship of the Thracian Wonder*. Modern Language Notes, vol. xxiii., 1908.

Hazlitt, William. *Lectures on the Dramatic Literature of the Age of Elizabeth*. 1821.

Hunt, Mary Leland. *Thomas Dekker*. Columbia University, 1911. [*v*. Appendix D.]

Kiesow, K. *Die verschiedenen Bearbeitungen der Novelle von der Herzogin von Amalfi des Bandello in den Literaturen des* xvi. *und* xvii. *Jahrhunderts*. 1895.

Lamb, Charles. *Specimens of the English Dramatic Poets*. 1808. 2nd Ed., 1813.

Lauschke, Johannes. *John Webster's Tragödie Appius and Virginia*. 1899.

Lee, Sidney. *John Webster*. Dictionary of National Biography, 1899.

Lowell, J. R. *The Old Dramatists*. Webster. 1892.

MacCracken, L. *A Page of Forgotten History*. 1911. (*i.e.* The Story of Vittoria.)

Meiners. Martin. *Metrische Untersuchungen über den*

Dramatiker, John Webster. 1893.

Michaelis, S. *The Admirable History of the Passion and Conversion of a Penitent Woman, seduced by a Magician.* 1613.

Murray, J. Tucker. *English Dramatic Companies,* 1585-1642. 2 vols., 1910.

Painter, W. *Palace of Pleasure.* 1566. Two volumes.

Pierce, F. E. *The Collaboration of Webster and Dekker.* 1909. Reviewed by Dr P. Aronstein in *Beiblatt zur Anglia,* 1910, p. 79.

Rieh, Barnabe. *New Descripton of Ireland.* 1610.

Scheffler, W. *Thomas Dekker als Dramatiker.* 1910.

Sidney, Sir Philip. *Arcadia.* 1590

Stoll, E. E. *John Webster. The Periods of his Work.* 1905. Reviewed by W. W. Greg in *Modern Language Review,* Oct. 1906.

Swinburne, A. C. *The Age of Shakespeare.* 1908. John Webster.

Swinburne, A. C. *Prologue to the Duchess of Malfy.* Nineteenth Century, 1899.

——*Studies in Prose and Poetry.* John Webster. 1894.

Symonds, J. A. *Italian Byways.* 1883. Vittoria Accoramboni. Reprinted in his *Studies in Italy and Greece.* Second Series.

The Repentance of Nathaniel Tindall that killed his mother. July 2, 1624.

A most bloody and unmatchable murder committed in Whitechapel by Nathaniel Tindall upon his own mother, written by John Morgan. (I cannot find either of these in the British Museum. They may not be extant.)

Vaughan, C. E. *Tourneur and Webster.* Article in Cambridge History of English Literature, vol. vi. Reviewed, Aronstein in *Beiblatt zur Anglia*, April 1911.

Vopel, C. *John Webster.* 1888.

Wurzbach, Wolfgang von. *Jahrbuch der deutschen Shakespeare-Gesellschaft.* 1898. John Webster.

Printed in Great Britain
by Amazon